BRITISH RAILWAYS POCKET BOOK No 1

LOCOMOTIVES

FORTY-THIRD EDITION
2001

The Complete Guide to all Diesel & Electric
Locomotives which operate on
the Railtrack & Eurotunnel Networks

Neil Webster

ISBN 1 902336 15 1

CONTENTS

Updates 2
Readers' Comments 2
Acknowledgements 3
Organisation & Operation of Britain's Railway System 3
Using This Book 6
General Information 9
Locomotives Authorised to Operate on the Railtrack Network
  1. Diesel Locomotives 12
  2. Electric & Electro-Diesel Locomotives 64
  3. Miscellaneous Vehicles 83
  4. Locomotives Awaiting Disposal 83
  5. Locomotives Undergoing Recertification 85
  6. Eurotunnel Locomotives 86
  7. Codes
    Livery Codes 89
    Owner Codes 91
    Pool Codes 92
    Depot, Works & Location Codes 94
    Depot Type Abbreviations 96

UPDATES

A comprehensive update to *Locomotives* is published every month in the Platform 5 magazine, *Today's Railways*, which also contains news and rolling stock information on the railways of both Britain and Continental Europe. This is the ONLY commercial magazine to contain official Platform 5 rolling stock updates. For further details of *Today's Railways,* please see the advertisements elsewhere within this book.

Information in this edition is intended to illustrate the actual situation on Britain's railways, rather than necessarily agree with TOPS, RSL and other computer records. Information is updated to 17 November 2000.

READERS' COMMENTS

With such a wealth of information as contained in this book, it is inevitable a few inaccuracies may be found. The author will be pleased to receive notification from readers of any such inaccuracies, and also of any additional information to supplement our records and thus enhance future editions.

Please send comments to Neil Webster, 312 Leeds Road, Birstall, Batley, West Yorkshire, WF17 0HS,

Tel: 01924 470235; Fax: 01924 473675; e-mail: neil.webster2@ntlworld.com

Special Note: Readers are advised that both the author and publisher regret they are unable to answer ANY specific locomotive and rolling stock queries (concerning the UK or elsewhere) other than through the 'Q & A' section in the Platform 5 magazine *Today's Railways*.

ACKNOWLEDGEMENTS

The author would like to thank the following companies and individuals for their help and co-operation with the compilation of this book:

English Welsh & Scottish Railway Ltd.
Enron Teesside Operations Ltd.
The Felixstowe Dock & Railway Company Ltd.
Freightliner Ltd.
Harry Needle Railroad Company Ltd.
Virgin Trains

Thanks are also due to the following individuals for their reports of changes observed during 2000:

Donald Bishop, Tony Booth, Graham Campbell, L. Clearie, Alan Costello, Les Forshaw, Keith Foster, Peter Fox, Ian Furness, Brian Garvin, David Haydock, M.J. Haywood, John Henley, Paul Jeffries, Kevin M. Lee, Dave Lewis, John Lewis, Paul Moore, Gordon Parrish, Tony Russell, John Salmon, David F. Smith, Alan Spencer, Alan Sugden, Bill Wise and Robert Volland, plus those who wish to remain anonymous.

ORGANISATION & OPERATION OF BRITAIN'S RAILWAY SYSTEM

INFRASTRUCTURE & OPERATION

Britain's national railway infrastructure (i.e. the track, signalling, stations and associated power supply equipment) is owned by a public company – Railtrack PLC. Many stations and maintenance depots are leased to and operated by Train Operating Companies (TOCs), but some larger stations remain under Railtrack control. The only exception is the infrastructure on the Isle of Wight, which is nationally owned and is leased to the Island Line franchisee.

Trains are operated by TOCs over the Railtrack network, regulated by access agreements between the parties involved. In general, TOCs are responsible for the provision and maintenance of the locomotives, rolling stock and staff necessary for the direct operation of services, whilst Railtrack is responsible for the provision and maintenance of the infrastructure and also for staff needed to regulate the operation of services.

DOMESTIC PASSENGER TRAIN OPERATORS

The large majority of passenger trains are operated by the TOCs on fixed term franchises. Franchise expiry dates are shown in parentheses in the list of franchisees below:

Franchise	Franchisee	Trading Name
Anglia Railways	GB Railways Ltd. (until 4 April 2004)	Anglia Railways
Cardiff Railway	National Express Group PLC (until 31 March 2001)	Cardiff Railways
Central Trains	National Express Group PLC (until 1 April 2004)	Central Trains
Chiltern Railways	M40 Trains Ltd. (until 20 July 2003)	Chiltern Railways
Cross Country	Virgin Rail Group Ltd. (until 4 January 2012)	Virgin Trains
Gatwick Express	National Express Group PLC (until 27 April 2011)	Gatwick Express
Great Eastern Railway	First Group PLC (until 4 April 2004)	First Great Eastern
Great Western Trains	First Group PLC (until 3 February 2006)	First Great Western
InterCity East Coast	GNER Holdings Ltd. (until 4 April 2004)	Great North Eastern Railway
InterCity West Coast	Virgin Rail Group Ltd. (until 8 March 2012)	Virgin Trains
Island Line	Stagecoach Holdings PLC (until 12 October 2001)	Island Line
LTS Rail	National Express Group PLC (until 25 May 2011)	C2C
Merseyrail Electrics	Arriva PLC (until 17 February 2001)	Merseyrail Electrics
Midland Main Line	National Express Group PLC (until 27 April 2008)	Midland Mainline
North London Railways	National Express Group PLC (until 1 September 2004)	Silverlink Train Services
North West Regional Railways	First Group PLC (until 1 April 2004)	First North Western
Regional Railways North East	Arriva PLC (until 17 February 2001)	Northern Spirit
Scotrail	National Express Group PLC (until 30 March 2004)	ScotRail
South Central	Connex Transport UK Ltd. (until 25 May 2003)	Connex
South Eastern	Connex Transport UK Ltd. (until 12 October 2011)	Connex
South Wales & West	National Express Group PLC (until 31 March 2001)	Wales & West Passenger Trains

South West	Stagecoach Holdings PLC (until 3 February 2003)	South West Trains
Thames	Victory Railways Holdings Ltd. (until 12 April 2004)	Thames Trains
Thameslink	GOVIA Ltd. (until 1 April 2004)	Thameslink Rail
Great Northern	National Express Group PLC (until 31 May 2001)	WAGN
West Anglia	National Express Group PLC (until 4 April 2004)	WAGN

Many of the shorter-term franchises are currently subject to re-negotiation. The Shadow Strategic Rail Authority has already announced M40 Trains Ltd. as preferred bidder for an extended Chiltern franchise, and GOVIA Ltd. as preferred bidder for replacement of the South Central franchise. Announcements regarding the future of other franchises were regarded as imminent as this edition closed for press.

The above companies may also operate other services under 'Open Access' arrangements.

The following operate non-franchised services only:

Operator	Trading Name	Route
British Airports Authority	Heathrow Express	London Paddington–Heathrow Airport
Hull Trains	Hull Trains	London King's Cross–Hull
West Coast Railway	West Coast Railway	Fort William–Mallaig

INTERNATIONAL PASSENGER OPERATIONS

Eurostar (UK) Ltd. operates international passenger-only services between the United Kingdom and continental Europe, jointly with French National Railways (SNCF) and Belgian National Railways (SNCB/NMBS). Eurostar (UK) is a subsidiary of London & Continental Railways Ltd., which is jointly owned by National Express Group plc and British Airways plc.

In addition, the tunnel operating company, Eurotunnel, provides a service for the conveyance of accompanied road vehicles through the Channel Tunnel.

FREIGHT TRAIN OPERATIONS

The following operators operate freight train services under 'Open Access' arrangements:

English Welsh & Scottish Railway Ltd. (EWS)
Freightliner Ltd.
GB Railfreight Ltd.
Direct Rail Services Ltd.
Mendip Rail Ltd.

USING THIS BOOK

LAYOUT OF INFORMATION

Railtrack registered locomotives are listed in numerical order of class number, and then in numerical order of individual locomotives – using current numbers as allocated by the Rolling Stock Library (RSL) – the national registry of rail vehicles. The only exceptions are locomotives numbered in the 89xxx series (see page 9), which are listed under their previous class numbers. Where numbers actually carried are different to those officially allocated, these are noted in class headings where appropriate. Where locomotives have been renumbered since the previous edition of this book, the most immediate previous number is shown in parentheses. Each locomotive entry is laid out as in one of the following examples:

Class 08 & 09 Shunting Locomotives

RSL No.	Detail	Livery	Owner	Pool	Depot	Location
08308 a	**SS**	RT	HASS	IS	*Inverness CARMD*

Official names carried are appended in a table following each class as appropriate.

Other Locomotives

RSL No.	Detail	Livery	Owner	Pool	Depot	Name
37682 r§	**E**	E	WKSN	TO	Hartlepool Pipe Mill

Eurotunnel locomotives are listed in numerical order of painted number. Each locomotive entry is laid out as in the following example:

No.	Detail	Livery	Owner	Depot	Name
9001	**ET**	ET	CO	LESLEY GARRETT

CLASS HEADINGS

Principal details and dimensions are quoted for each class in metric and/or imperial units as considered appropriate bearing in mind common UK usage. The following abbreviations are used:

a.c.	alternating current.
BR	British Railways.
d.c.	direct current.
H-B	Hunslet-Barclay.
h.p.	horse power.
HNRC	Harry Needle Railroad Company
Hz	Hertz.
KN	kilonewtons.
km/h	kilometres per hour.
kW	kilowatts.
lbf	ponds force

m.	metres.
mm.	millimetres.
m.p.h.	miles per hour.
RCH	Railway Clearing House.
r.p.m.	revolutions per minute.
RR	Rolls Royce.
RSL	Rolling Stock Library.
SR	Southern Region
t.	tonnes.
TDM	Time Division Multiplex.
TE	Tractive Effort.
V	Volts.

All dimensions and weights are quoted for locomotives in an 'as new' condition with all necessary supplies (e.g. oil, water and sand) on board. Dimensions are quoted in the order Length – Width – Height. Lengths quoted are over buffers or couplings as appropriate. All width and height dimensions quoted are maxima. For overhead supply system electric locomotives, the height quoted is with pantograph lowered. Where two different wheel diameter dimensions are shown, the first refers to powered wheels and the second refers to non-powered wheels.

DETAIL DIFFERENCES

Only detail differences which currently affect the areas and types of train which locomotives may work are shown. All other detail differences are specifically excluded. Where such differences occur within a class or part class, they are shown in the 'Detail' column alongside the individual locomotive number. Standard abbreviations used are:

a	Train air brake equipment only.
b	Buckeye couplers.
c	Scharfenberg couplers.
j	RCH jumper cables for operating with Propelling Control Vehicles.
k	Swinghead automatic knuckle couplers.
p	Train air, vacuum and electro-pneumatic brakes.
r	Radio Electronic Token Block (RETB) equipment.
s	Slow Speed Control equipment.
v	Train vacuum brake only.
x	Train air and vacuum brakes ('Dual brakes').
+	Additional fuel tank capacity.
§	Sandite laying equipment.

In all cases use of the above abbreviations indicates the equipment indicated is normally operable. Meaning of non-standard abbreviations and symbols is detailed in individual class headings.

LIVERY CODES

Livery codes are used to denote the various liveries carried. It is impossible in a publication of this size to list every livery variation which currently exists. In particular items ignored for the purposes of this publication include:

- Minor colour variations.
- Omission of logos.
- All numbering, lettering and branding.

Descriptions quoted are thus a general guide only. Logos as appropriate for each livery are normally deemed to be carried. A complete list of livery codes used appears on pages 89–91.

OWNER CODES

Owner codes are used to denote the owners of locomotives listed. A complete list of owner codes used appears on pages 91–92.

POOL CODES

Locomotives are split into operational groups ('pools') for diagramming and maintenance purposes. The official codes used to denote these pools are shown in this publication. A complete list of pool codes used appears on pages 92–94.

DEPOT & LOCATION CODES

Depot codes are used in this publication to denote the normal maintenance base of each operational locomotive (except Freightliner operated locomotives). However, maintenance may be carried out at other locations and may also be carried out by mobile maintenance teams.

The codes FD and FE are used for locomotives operated by Freightliner. This company does not operate a depot based maintenance system for its locomotives, instead using mobile maintenance teams to carry out day-to-day maintenance, with heavier repairs being performed by contractors.

Location codes are used to denote the current actual location of stored vehicles. A location code will always be followed by (S) to denote stored.

A complete list of depot and location codes used appears on pages 94–96.

A complete list of the abbreviations used to denote different types of depots appears on page 96.

SHUNTING LOCOMOTIVE LOCATIONS

The actual location of operational shunting locomotives of classes 08 & 09, updated to reports received as at 17 November 2000, is included as a guide to readers as to where these locomotives may be found. Whilst some locomotives remain at certain locations for considerable lengths of time, others may move around far more frequently. Readers must appreciate the listing of a locomotive at a location is no absolute guarantee the locomotive concerned (or any other locomotive) will remain present on a subsequent date.

NAMES

Only names carried with official sanction are listed in this publication. As far as possible names are shown in UPPER/lower case characters as actually shown on the name carried on the locomotive. Names known to be carried on one side only are suffixed [1] (e.g. Back Tor[1]).

GENERAL INFORMATION

CLASSIFICATION AND NUMBERING

All locomotives are classified and allocated numbers by the Rolling Stock Library under the TOPS numbering system, introduced in 1972. This comprises a two-digit class number followed by a three-digit serial number. Where the actual number carried by a locomotive differs from the allocated number, or where an additional number is carried to the allocated number, this is shown by a note in the class heading.

For diesel locomotives, class numbers offer an indication of engine horsepower as shown in the table below.

Class No. Range	Engine h.p.
01–14	0–799
15–20	800–1000
21–31	1001–1499
32–39	1500–1999
40–54, 57	2000–2999
55–56, 58–69	3000+

For electric locomotives class numbers are allocated in ascending numerical order under the following scheme:

Class 70–80   direct current and d.c./diesel dual system locomotives.
Class 81 onwards   alternating current and a.c./d.c. dual system locos.

Numbers in the 89xxx series (except 89001) are allocated by the Rolling Stock Library to locomotives which have been de-registered but subsequently re-registered for use on the Railtrack network and whose original number has already been re-used. 89xxx numbers are normally only carried inside locomotive cabs and are not carried externally in normal circumstances.

WHEEL ARRANGEMENT

For main line locomotives the system whereby the number of driven axles on a bogie or frame is denoted by a letter (A = 1, B = 2, C = 3 etc.) and the number of non-powered axles is denoted by a number is used. The use of the letter 'o' after a letter indicates each axle is individually powered, whilst the + symbol indicates bogies are inter-coupled.

For shunting locomotives, the Whyte notation is used. In this notation the number of leading wheels are given, followed by the number of driving wheels and then the trailing wheels.

HAULAGE CAPABILITY OF DIESEL LOCOMOTIVES

The haulage capability of a diesel locomotive depends upon three basic factors:

1. Adhesive weight. The greater the weight on the driving wheels, the greater the adhesion and more tractive power can be applied before wheelslip occurs.

2. The characteristics of its transmission. To start a train the locomotive has to exert a pull at standstill. A direct drive diesel engine cannot do this, hence the need for transmission. This may be mechanical, hydraulic or electric. The present British Standard for locomotives is electric transmission. Here the diesel engine drives a generator or alternator and the current produced is fed to the traction motors. The force produced by each driven wheel depends on the current in its traction motor. In other words, the larger the current, the harder it pulls. As the locomotive speed increases, the current in the traction motor falls, hence the *Maximum Tractive Effort* is the maximum force at its wheels the locomotive can exert at a standstill. The electrical equipment cannot take such high currents for long without overheating. Hence the *Continuous Tractive Effort* is quoted which represents the current which the equipment can take continuously.

3. The power of its engine. Not all power reaches the rail, as electrical machines are approximately 90% efficient. As the electrical energy passes through two such machines (the generator or alternator and the traction motors), the *Power at Rail* is approximately 81% (90% of 90%) of the engine power, less a further amount used for auxiliary equipment such as radiator fans, traction motor blowers, air compressors, battery charging, cab heating, Electric Train Supply (ETS) etc. The power of the locomotive is proportional to the tractive effort times the speed. Hence when on full power there is a speed corresponding to the continuous tractive effort.

HAULAGE CAPABILITY OF ELECTRIC LOCOMOTIVES

Unlike a diesel locomotive, an electric locomotive does not develop it power on board and its performance is determined only by two factors, namely its weight and the characteristics of its electrical equipment. Whereas a diesel locomotive tends to be a constant power machine, the power of an electric locomotive varies considerably. Up to a certain speed it can produce virtually a constant tractive effort. Hence power rises with speed according to the formula given in section three above, until a maximum speed is reached at which tractive effort falls, such that the power also falls. Hence the power at the speed corresponding to the maximum tractive effort is lower than the maximum speed.

BRAKE FORCE

The brake force is a measure of the braking power of a locomotive. This is shown on the locomotive data panels so operating staff can ensure sufficient brake power is available on freight trains.

ELECTRIC TRAIN SUPPLY (ETS)

A number of locomotives are equipped to provide a supply of electricity to the train being hauled to power auxiliaries such as heating, cooling fans, air conditioning and kitchen equipment. ETS is provided from the locomotive by means of a separate alternator (except Class 33 locos, which have a dc generator). The ETS index of a locomotive is a measure of the electrical power available for train supply.

Similarly, most loco-hauled coaches also have an ETS index, which in this case is a measure of the power required to operate equipment mounted in the coach. The sum of the ETS indices of all the hauled vehicles in a train must not exceed the ETS index of the locomotive.

ETS is commonly (but incorrectly) known as ETH (Electric Train Heating), which term is a throwback to the days before loco-hauled coaches were equipped with electrically powered auxiliary equipment other than for train heating.

ROUTE AVAILABILITY (RA)

This is a measure of a railway vehicle's axle load. The higher the axle load of a vehicle, the higher the RA number on a scale from 1 to 10. Each Railtrack route has a RA number and in general no vehicle with a higher RA number may travel on that route without special clearance. A map showing route availability on all routes is published on the Railtrack internet web site.

MULTIPLE & PUSH-PULL WORKING

Multiple working between vehicles (i.e. two or more powered vehicles being driven from one cab) is facilitated by jumper cables connecting the vehicles. However, not all types are compatible with each other, and a number of different systems are in use, each system being incompatible with any other.

Association of American Railroads (AAR) System: Classes 59, 66, and 67.
Blue Star Coupling Code: Classes 20, 25, 31, 33, and 37. Locomotives 47971 and 47972.
Green Circle Coupling Code: Class 47 (not all equipped).
Orange Square Coupling Code: Class 50.
Red Diamond Coupling Code: Classes 56 and 58.
SR System: Classes 33/1, 73 and various EMUs.
Within Own Class only: Classes 43 and 60.

Class 47 locos 47701–47717 use a time-division multiplex (TDM) system for push-pull working which utilises the existing Railway Clearing House (RCH) jumper cables fitted to coaching stock vehicles. Previously these cables had only been used to control train lighting and public address systems.

A number of other locomotives are equipped with a more modern TDM system for push-pull working which also facilitates multiple working.

LOCOMOTIVES AUTHORISED TO OPERATE ON THE RAILTRACK NETWORK

1. DIESEL LOCOMOTIVES

SERIES 01/5   BARCLAY/RR   0–6–0

Built: 1985–86 by Andrew Barclay at Kilmarnock (Works Nos. 663 & 668 respectively), for the Ministry of Defence Army Department (Nos. 626 and 631 respectively). Registered for use on the Railtrack network in 1999. Loading gauge restrictions preclude use of these locomotives other than between Kineton and Fenny Compton.
Engine: Rolls Royce CV12TCE of 445 kW (600 h.p.) at ? r.p.m.
Transmission: Hydraulic.
Maximum Tractive Effort:
Continuous Tractive Effort:
Brake Force: 46 t.
Weight: 61.0 t.
Design Speed: 60 km/h.
Fuel Capacity: 3000 litres.
Train Supply: Not equipped.

Train Brakes: Air.
Dimensions: 9.45 x ? x ? m.
Wheel Diameter:
Maximum Speed: 10 m.p.h.
RA: 7.
Multiple Working: Not equipped.

01505	**MD** MD	MBDL	KN	
01506	**MD** MD	MBDL	KN	

SERIES 01/5   H-B/CATERPILLAR   0–6–0

Built: 1971 by The Hunslet Engine Company at Leeds (Works No. 7018), for the National Coal Board, Western Area (No. 8D). Subsequently sold to Hunslet-Barclay, Kilmarnock and rebuilt prior to sale to The Felixstowe Dock and Railway Company in 1999. Registered for use on the Railtrack network in 1999. Normally used at Felixstowe South Container Terminal.
Engine: Caterpillar 3412C DITA of 475 kW (640 h.p.) at ? r.p.m.
Transmission: Hydraulic. Twin Disc 13800 series torque converter coupled to a Hunslet final drive.
Maximum Tractive Effort: 180 kN (40365 lbf).
Continuous Tractive Effort: 235 kN (52700 lbf) at ?? m.p.h.
Train Brakes: Air.
Brake Force: 48 t.
Weight: 64.3 t.
Design Speed: 15 m.p.h.
Fuel Capacity: 930 litres.
Train Supply: Not equipped.

Dimensions: 3.95 x 2.51 x 3.80 m.
Wheel Diameter: 1143 mm.
Maximum Speed: 15 m.p.h.
RA: 7.
Multiple Working: Not equipped.

Non standard numbering: 01531 also carries number H4323.

01531	**FX** FX	MBDL	FX	COLONEL TOMLINE

SERIES 01/5   ENGLISH ELECTRIC/RR   0–4–0

Built: 1966 by English Electric at Vulcan Foundry, Newton le Willows (Works No. D1122), for the Central Electricity Generating Board at Croydon 'B' Power Station (No. 2). Subsequently acquired by RFS(E), Doncaster (now Wabtec). Registered for use on the Railtrack network in 2000, and hired to Aggregate Industries UK for use at Croft Quarry, Leicestershire.
Engine: ? of 235 kW (315 h.p.) at ? r.p.m.
Transmission: Hydraulic.
Maximum Tractive Effort:
Continuous Tractive Effort:
Train Brakes: Air.
Brake Force: 10 t.   **Dimensions:** 7.32 x ? x ? m.
Weight: 24.0 t.   **Wheel Diameter:**
Design Speed: 10 m.p.h.   **Maximum Speed:** 10 m.p.h.
Fuel Capacity: 1365 litres.   **RA:** 0.
Train Supply: Not equipped.   **Multiple Working:** Not equipped.
Non standard livery:
• 01551 is in RFS(E) livery of blue, lined out in silver.

01551   **0**   WA   MBDL   ZB

SERIES 01/5   HNRC/RR   0–6–0

Built: 1966 by Thomas Hill at Vanguard Works, Kilnhurst (Works No. 167V), for ICI Billingham (No. D3). Subsequently sold to Harry Needle Railroad Company in 1995 and rebuilt 2000. Registered for use on the Railtrack network in 2000, and hired to Creative Logistics, for use at Salford International Railfreight Terminal.
Engine: Rolls Royce 8-cylinder of 275 kW (370 h.p.) at ? r.p.m.
Transmission: Hydraulic. Twin Disc 11800 torque converter coupled to a RF final drive unit.
Maximum Tractive Effort:
Continuous Tractive Effort:
Train Brakes: Air.
Brake Force: 19 t.   **Dimensions:** 9.14 x ? x ? m.
Weight: 49.0 t.   **Wheel Diameter:**
Design Speed: 10 m.p.h.   **Maximum Speed:** 10 m.p.h.
Fuel Capacity: 1360 litres.   **RA:** 5.
Train Supply: Not equipped.   **Multiple Working:** Not equipped.
Non standard livery:
• 01552 is in Creative Logistics livery of blue and green.

01552   **0**   HN   HNRL   BH

CLASS 03   BR/GARDNER   0–6–0

Built: 1962 by BR at Swindon Works. Normally used at Hornsey T&RSMD.
Engine: Gardner 8L3 of 152 kW (204 h.p.) at 1200 r.p.m.

Transmission: Mechanical. Fluidrive type 23 hydraulic coupling to Wilson-Drewry CA5R7 gearbox with SCG type RF11 final drive.
Maximum Tractive Effort: 68 kN (15300 lbf).
Continuous Tractive Effort: 68 kN (15300 lbf) at 3.75 m.p.h.
Train Brakes: Air & vacuum.

Brake Force: 13 t.	**Dimensions:** 7.93 x 2.59 x 3.73 m.
Weight: 31.3 t.	**Wheel Diameter:** 1092 mm.
Design Speed: 28.5 m.p.h.	**Maximum Speed:** 28.5 m.p.h.
Fuel Capacity: 1364 litres.	**RA:** 1.
Train Supply: Not equipped.	**Multiple Working:** Not equipped.

03179   **WN** WN   HQXX   HE   CLIVE

CLASS 08   BR/ENGLISH ELECTRIC   0–6–0

Built: 1955–62 by BR at Crewe, Darlington, Derby, Doncaster or Horwich Works.
Engine: English Electric 6KT of 298 kW (400 h.p.) at 680 r.p.m.
Main Generator: English Electric 801.
Traction Motors: Two English Electric 506.
Maximum Tractive Effort: 156 kN (35000 lbf).
Continuous Tractive Effort: 49 kN (11100 lbf) at 8.8 m.p.h.

Power At Rail: 194 kW (260 h.p.).	**Train Brakes:** Air & vacuum.
Brake Force: 19 t.	**Dimensions:** 8.92 x 2.59 x 3.89 m.
Weight: 49.6–50.4 t.	**Wheel Diameter:** 1372 mm.
Design Speed: 20 m.p.h.	**Maximum Speed:** 15 m.p.h.
Fuel Capacity: 3037 litres.	**RA:** 5.
Train Supply: Not equipped.	**Multiple Working:** Not equipped.

Non-standard liveries/numbering:
* 08397 is as **F**, but with BR Railfreight General yellow & red logos.
* 08414 is as **DG**, but with BR & Railfreight Distribution logos and large bodyside numbers. Also carries number D3529.
* 08460 is light grey with black underframe, cab doors, window surrounds and roof. Also carries number D3575.
* 08500 is red, lined out in black and white. Also carries a large number '1' on the bodyside.
* 08527 is light grey with a black roof, blue bodyside stripe and 'Ilford Level 5' branding,
* 08573 is light grey and unnumbered.
* 08593 is Great Eastern Railway style blue. Also carries number D3760.
* 08601 is London Midland & Scottish Railway style black.
* 08616 carries number 3783.
* 08617 is in Virgin Trains 'Pitstop' livery of black with a large red and black bodyside flag.
* 08642 is London & South Western Railway style black. Also carries number D3809.
* 08649 is grey with blue, white and red stripes and WTL logo. Also carries number D3816.
* 08682 is dark blue with a grey roof.
* 08715 is 'Dayglo' orange.
* 08721 is as **B**, but with a red and yellow stripe.
* 08834 is in RFS(E) livery of blue with silver lining.

- 08730/867 are in plain black livery.
- 08785 is silver grey.
- 08801 carries number 801.
- 08805 is London Midland & Scottish Railway style maroon. Also carries number 3973.
- 08809 is light grey with orange lettering.
- 08879 is green and black with Railfreight Distribution logos.
- 08883 is Caledonian Railway style blue.
- 08928 is as **FO**, with large bodyside numbers and light blue solebar.

Notes: † – Equipped with remote control (Hima Sella system) for working at Allied Steel & Wire, Cardiff.

‡ – Equipped with remote control (Cattron system) for evaluation purposes.

Class 08/0. Standard Design.

08077	**RF**	P	DFLS	FD	*Southampton Millbrook Freightliner Terminal*
08308 a	**SS**	RT	HASS	IS	*Inverness CARMD*
08331	**GN**	WA	RFSH	EC	*Craigentinny T&RSMD*
08375 a	**RT**	RT	DFLS	FD	*Ipswich Yard*
08389	**B**	EF	WSXX	OC(S)	
08393 a	**FE**	EF	WSSE	OC	*Ripple Lane Yard*
08397 a	**0**	E	WSWM	BS	*Padeswood Hall Cement Works*
08401 a	**DG**	E	WSYH	IM	*Scunthorpe Trent Yard*
08402 a	**DG**	E	WSXX	BK(S)	
08405 a	**DG**	E	WSYH	IM	*Immingham TMD*
08410 a	**GL**	FW	HJSL	LA	*Laira T&RSMD*
08411 a	**B**	E	WSSC	ML	*Falkland Yard*
08414 a	**0**	E	WSWX	OC(S)	
08417 a	**B**	SO	XYPS	MD	*Merehead*
08418 a	**F**	E	WSWM	BS	*Blue Circle Cement, Washwood Heath*
08428 a	**E**	E	WSYH	IM	*Doncaster TMD*
08441 a	**B**	E	WSSC	ML	*Ayr WRD*
08442 a	**F**	E	WSYH	IM	*Immingham Dock*
08451	**B**	VW	HFSN	WN	*Willesden TMD*
08454	**VP**	VW	HFSN	WN	*Willesden TMD*
08460 a	**0**	E	WSNW	AN	*Guide Bridge Brookside Sidings*
08466 a†	**E**	E	WSAW	CF	*Cardiff Rod Mill*
08472 a	**BR**	WA	RFSH	EC	*Craigentinny T&RSMD*
08480 a	**G**	E	WSSW	CF	*Did.c.ot Yard*
08481	**B**	E	WSAW	CF	*Cardiff Docks*
08482 a	**FD**	E	WSSE	OC	*Old Oak Common TMD*
08483 a	**GL**	FW	HJXX	PM	*St. Phillips Marsh T&RSMD*
08484	**DG**	RC	KWSW	ZN	*Railcare, Wolverton*
08485 a	**B**	EF	WSNW	AN	*Allerton T&RS TMD*
08489 a	**F**	E	WSWX	WA(S)	
08492 a	**B**	E	WSSC	ML	*Motherwell T&RSMD*
08493 a	**B**	E	WSXX	CF(S)	
08495	**E**	E	WSYH	IM	Worksop Yards
08499 a	**F**	E	WSXX	KY(S)	
08500	**0**	E	WSWS	EH	*Bristol Barton Hill T&RSMD*
08506 a	**B**	E	WSWX	OC(S)	

08509 a	**F**	E	WSWX	IM(S)	
08510 a	**B**	E	WSYH	IM	*Doncaster Wood Yard*
08511 a	**E**	E	WSEM	TO	*Toton Up Yard*
08512 a	**F**	E	WSYH	IM	*Doncaster Royal Mail Terminal*
08514 a	**B**	E	WSYH	IM	*Worksop Yards*
08516 a	**DG**	E	WSEM	TO	*Peterborough Yards*
08523	**ML**	E	WSXX	CD(S)	
08525	**F**	MA	HISL	NL	*Neville Hill (InterCity)T&RSMD*
08526	**E**	E	WSSE	OC	*Dagenham Dock Up Sidings*
08527	**0**	AD	KCSI	ZI	*Adtranz, Ilford*
08528	**DG**	E	WSEM	TO	*Castle Cement, Ketton*
08529	**B**	E	WSXX	DR(S)	
08530	**DG**	P	DFLS	FD	*Felixstowe North Container Terminal*
08531 a	**DG**	P	DFLS	FD	*Stratford SD*
08534	**DG**	E	WSSC	ML	*Mossend Yard*
08535	**DG**	EF	WSXX	CD(S)	
08536	**B**	MA	HISE	DY(S)	
08538	**DG**	E	WSEM	TO	*Toton TMD*
08540	**DG**	E	WSWM	BS	*Crewe Diesel TMD*
08541	**DG**	E	WSWX	OC(S)	
08542	**F**	E	WSXX	BS(S)	
08543	**DG**	E	WSWM	BS	*Saltley SD*
08561	**B**	E	WSNW	AN	
08567	**B**	E	WSWM	BS	*Allerton T&RSMD*
08568 a	**B**	RC	KGSS	ZH(S)	
08569	**E**	EF	WSEM	TO	*Peterborough Yards*
08571 a	**B**	WA	RFSH	EC	*Craigentinny T&RSMD*
08573	**0**	AD	KCSI	ZI	*Adtranz, Ilford*
08575	**B**	P	DFLS	FD	*Southampton Millbrook Freightliner Terminal*
08576	**B**	E	WSXX	CF(S)	
08577	**B**	E	WSNE	TE	*Tyne Yard*
08578	**RG**	E	WSNW	AN	*Trafford Park Freight Terminal*
08580	**B**	E	WSWM	BS	*Northampton Castle Yard*
08582 a	**DG**	E	WSNE	TE	*Thornaby TMD*
08585	**B**	P	DFLS	FD	*Trafford Park Container Terminal*
08587	**B**	E	WSYH	IM	*Wabtec, Doncaster*
08588	**BR**	MA	HISL	NL(S)	
08593	**0**	E	WSSE	OC	*Old Oak Common TMD*
08596 a†	**WA**	WA	RFSH	ZB	*Leeds Station*
08597	**B**	E	WSYH	IM	*Healey Mills Yard*
08599	**B**	E	WSNW	AN	*Peak Forest Sorting Sidings*
08601	**0**	E	WSXX	AN(S)	
08605	**B**	E	WSYH	IM	*Knottingley T&RSMD*
08611	**V**	VW	HFSL	LO	*Longsight T&RSMD*
08616	**GW**	MA	HGSS	TS	*Soho T&RSMD*
08617	**0**	VW	HFSN	WN	*Willesden TMD*
08623	**B**	E	WSWM	BS	*Wolverhampton Steel Terminal*
08624	**B**	P	DFLS	FD	*Fragonset, Derby*
08628	**B**	E	WSXX	SY(S)	
08629	**RP**	RC	KWSW	ZN	*Railcare, Wolverton*

▲ One of a number of shunters recently registered for use on Railtrack metals in the 01xxx series, No. 01531 is pictured at the Port of Felixstowe on 19th February 2000. **John Day**

▼ West Anglia Great Northern (WAGN) Railway liveried Class 03 No. 03179 'CLIVE' is pictured at the WAGN depot at Hornsey on 15th June 1999.
Ross Aitken

▲ Class 08 No. 08393, carrying Railfreight Distribution livery, is pictured passing through Stratford on 4th December 1999.　　　**K. Conkey**

▼ English Welsh & Scottish Railway liveried Class 08 No. 08995 stands at Margam Yard on 28th June 2000.　　　**Rodney Lissenden**

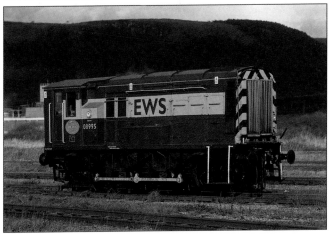

▲ Carrying EWS livery but without the branding, Class 09 No. 09009 'Three Bridges CED' stands at Harwich Parkeston Yard on 1st October 2000. **Alan Sargeant**

▼ Direct Rail Services liveried Class 20 No. 20309 is pictured nose first at Leiston, East Suffolk after arriving with a nuclear flask wagon from Sellafield. The date is 26th August 1999. **Michael J. Collins**

▲ A pair of Fragonset Railways livered Class 31s, Nos. 31601 'BLETCHLEY PARK 'STATION X'' and 31602 'CHIMAERA', pass Dore with a return Skegness–Derby charter on 15th July 2000. **Peter Fox**

▼ One of only two Class 33s in service with EWS, Civil-link liveried No. 33025 stands at Aberdeen Guild Street Yard on 31st May 2000. **G.W. Morrison**

▲ Loadhaul liveried Class 37 No. 37713 passes Bell Veu with a Ditton to Immingham Maritime Intermodal train on 26th March 1999.　**Ian A. Lyall**

▼ The 06.45 Newcastle–Plymouth, led by Virgin Trains liveried Class 43 Power Car No. 43084 'County of Derbyshire', runs along the sea wall at Horse Cove, Dawlish on 4th March 2000.　**John Chalcraft**

▲ BR Green Class 46 No. D 172 'Ixion' hauls three preserved locos and support coach through Oxford station on 4th August 2000. All four locos were en-route to Old Oak Common, where they exhibited at the open weekend held there on the 5th/6th August 2000. **Darren Ford**

▼ Still carrying the obsolescent Intercity livery, Class 47 No. 47805 enters Kensington Olympia with the 07.17 Manchester Piccadilly–Brighton service on 26th February 2000. **David Brown**

▲ First Great Western liveried Class 47 No. 47813 'SS Great Britain' hurries past Marazion on 13th July 2000 with the 12.52 Penzance–London Paddington.

John Chalcraft

▼ Class 50 No. 50017 carries a livery similar to one used by the LMS for the locomotives which worked the 'Coronation Scot' service. It is pictured here at Yate with the 17.06 Bath Spa–Manchester Piccadilly return charter on 22nd July 2000.

John Chalcraft

▲ BR blue Class 55 No. 55019 'ROYAL HIGHLAND FUSILIER' passes Normanton with a charter special on 8th September 1999.　　**G.W. Morrison**

▼ Transrail Freight liveried Class 56 No. 56079 hauls a Falkland Yard to Carlisle coal train past Troon Golf Course, Ayrshire on 28th April 1999.　　**Paul Senior**

08630	E	E	WSSC	ML	Motherwell T&RSMD
08631	N	PO	HSSN	NC	*Norwich Crown Point T&RSMD*
08632	B	E	WSXX	CD(S)	
08633	RX	E	WSNE	TE	*Thornaby TMD*
08635	B	E	WSSE	OC	*Dagenham Dock Up Sidings*
08641	DG	FW	HJSL	LA	*Plymouth Station*
08642	O	P	DFLS	ST(S)	
08643	GL	FW	HJXX	PM	*St. Phillips Marsh T&RSMD*
08644	IM	FW	HJSL	LA	*Penzance*
08645	DG	FW	HJSL	LA	*Laira T&RSMD*
08646	F	E	WSWS	EH	*Eastleigh Yards*
08648	DG	FW	HJSL	LA(S)	
08649	O	AM	KESE	ZG	*Alstom, Eastleigh*
08651	DG	E	WSSW	CF	*Cardiff Canton TMD*
08653	FE	EF	WSWS	EH	*Bristol Barton Hill T&RSMD*
08655	F	EF	WSYH	IM	*Knottingley T&RSMD*
08661 a	F	EF	WSYX	AN(S)	
08662	B	E	WSYH	IM	*Tinsley Yard*
08663 a	GL	FW	HJSL	LA	*Plymouth Station*
08664	E	E	WSWS	EH	*Westbury Yard*
08665	B	E	WSYH	IM	*Immingham TMD*
08666	B	E	WSYX	AN(S)	
08670 a	B	E	WSSC	ML	*Wabtec, Doncaster*
08673	IM	E	WSYX	AN(S)	
08675	F	E	WSXX	ML(S)	
08676	B	E	WSYH	IM	*Hull King George Dock*
08682	O	AD	KDSD	ZF	*Adtranz, Doncaster*
08683	B	E	WSWM	BS	*Bescot TMD*
08685	B	E	WSSC	ML	*Polmadie T&RSMD*
08689 a	E	E	WSYH	IM	*Immingham Reception Sidings*
08690	MA	MA	HISE	DY	*Etches Park T&RSMD*
08691	G	WA	DFLS	FD	*Crewe Diesel TMD*
08694 a	E	EF	WSSE	OC	*Wembley Yards*
08695 a	E	E	WSWM	BS	*Wolverhampton Steel Terminal*
08696 a	V	VW	HFSL	LO	*Liverpool Downhill CSD*
08697	B	MA	HISE	DY(S)	
08698 a	E	E	WSWM	BS	*Daventry International Railfreight Terminal*
08701 a	RX	E	WSNW	AN	*Warrington Yards*
08702	B	E	WSXX	ZB(S)	
08703 a	B	EF	WSNW	AN	*Warrington Yards*
08706	B	E	WSEM	TO	*Toton Up Yard*
08709	B	E	WSNW	AN	*Carlisle Kingmoor Yard*
08711	RX	E	WSSE	OC	*Stratford SD*
08714	RX	E	WSEM	TO	*Peterborough Yards*
08715 v	O	E	WSXX	SF(S)	
08720	E	E	WSSC	ML	*Mossend Yard*
08721	O	VW	HFSL	LO	*Longsight T&RSMD*
08724	WA	WA	RFSH	ZB	*Leeds Neville Hill*
08730	O	RC	KGSS	ZH	*Railcare, Glasgow*
08735	DG	E	WSWX	DR(S)	
08737 a	FE	EF	WSNW	AN	*Trafford Park Freight Terminal*

08738	**E**	E	WSWM	BS	*Crewe Diesel TMD*
08739	**B**	EF	WSXX	AN(S)	
08740	**F**	E	WSXX	SF(S)	
08742	**RX**	E	WSWM	BS	*Longport Sidings*
08743	**EN**	EN	MBDL	BG	*ICI, Billingham*
08745	**FE**	P	DFLS	CD(S)	
08746	**DG**	E	WSXX	DR(S)	
08750	**B**	RT	KESE	ZG	Alstom, Eastleigh
08751	**F**	EF	WSXX	ZB(S)	
08752 †	**CE**	E	WSAW	CF	*Sheerness Dockyard*
08754	**FL**	RT	DFLS	FD	*Garston Freightliner Terminal*
08756	**DG**	E	WSXX	CF(S)	
08757	**E**	E	WSEM	TO	*Toton TMD*
08758	**B**	E	WSXX	SF(S)	
08762	**B**	RT	DFLS	FD	*Dagenham Dock Up Sidings*
08765	**DG**	E	WSWM	BS	*Hams Hall Freight Terminal*
08768	**B**	E	WSYX	ML(S)	
08770 a	**DG**	E	WSAW	CF	*Allied Steel & Wire, Cardiff*
08775	**E**	E	WSSE	OC	*Old Oak Common TMD*
08776 a	**DG**	E	WSSE	OC	*Sherness Dockyard*
08780	**B**	FW	HJSE	LE	*Landore T&RSMD*
08782 a	**B**	E	WSXX	CD(S)	
08783	**B**	E	WSYH	IM	*Wabtec, Doncaster*
08784	**B**	EF	WSNW	AN	*Warrington Yards*
08785 a	**O**	P	DFLS	FD	*Crewe Basford Hall Yard*
08786 a	**DG**	E	WSWS	EH	*Eastleigh T&RSMD*
08788	**RT**	RT	HASS	IS	*Inverness T&RSMD*
08790	**B**	VW	HFSL	LO	*Longsight T&RSMD*
08792	**T**	E	WSSW	CF	*Onllwyn*
08795	**IM**	FW	HJSE	LE	*Landore T&RSMD*
08798	**B**	E	WSWS	EH	*Tavistock Junction*
08799	**B**	EF	WSSE	OC	*Old Oak Common TMD*
08801	**B**	E	WSXX	CF(S)	
08802	**RX**	E	WSWM	BS	*Crewe Diesel TMD*
08804	**B**	E	WSWS	EH	*Eastleigh Yards*
08805	**O**	MA	HGSS	TS	*Tyseley T&RSMD*
08806 a	**F**	E	WSNE	TE	*Thornaby TMD*
08807	**BR**	E	WSSC	ML	*Killoch Disposal Point*
08809	**O**	HN	DFLS	FD	*Coatbridge Freightliner Terminal*
08810 a	**AR**	AR	HSSN	NC	*Norwich Crown Point T&RSMD*
08813 a	**DG**	E	WSYX	TE(S)	
08815	**B**	E	WSYX	AN(S)	
08817	**BR**	E	WSXX	AN(S)	
08818	**B**	HN	DFLS	FD	*Crewe Basford Hall Yard*
08819	**DG**	E	WSXX	CF(S)	
08822	**GL**	FW	HJXX	PM	*Old Oak Common HST Depot*
08823 a	**B**	AD	KDSD	ZF	*Adtranz, Doncaster*
08824 a	**F**	E	WSYH	IM	*Immingham Reception Sidings*
08825 a	**B**	EF	WSXX	OC(S)	
08827 a	**B**	E	WSYX	ML(S)	
08828 a	**E**	E	WSSW	CF	*Wabtec, Doncaster*

08830	LW	CA	HLSV	CP	*Crewe Carriage Depot*
08834	O	WA	RFSH	BN	*Bounds Green T&RSMD*
08836	IM	FW	HJXX	OO	*Old Oak Common HST Depot*
08837	DG	EF	WSXX	AN(S)	
08842	B	EF	WSNW	AN	*Allerton T&RSMD*
08844	B	EF	WSYH	IM	*Doncaster TMD*
08847	B	AM	KESE	ZG(S)	
08853 a	B	WA	RFSH	ZB	*Wabtec, Doncaster*
08854 †	E	E	WSAW	CF	*Cardiff Canton TMD*
08856	B	EF	WSWS	EH	*Cardiff Canton TMD*
08865	B	E	WSSE	OC	*Old Oak Common TMD*
08866	B	E	WSWM	BS	*Dee Marsh Sidings*
08867	O	E	WSXX	DE(S)	
08868	B	HN	DFLS	FD	*Crewe Basford Hall Yard*
08869	G	AR	HSSN	NC(S)	
08870	RL	RL	MBDL	DE	*Brunner-Mond, Northwich*
08872	DG	EF	WSSE	OC	*Old Oak Common TMD*
08873	RX	RT	MBDL	CP	*Crewe Carriage Depot*
08874	SL	RT	H.P.XX	BY	*Bletchley T&RSMD*
08877	DG	E	WSWX	SP(S)	
08879	O	EF	WSYH	IM	*Doncaster Up Yard*
08880	B	E	WSXX	AN(S)	
08881	DG	E	WSSC	ML	*Ayr SD*
08882	B	E	WSSC	ML	*Falkland Yard*
08883	O	E	WSSC	ML	*Perth Yard*
08884	B	E	WSWM	BS	*Washwood Heath Yard*
08886 ‡	E	E	WSYH	IM	*Immingham Reception Sidings*
08887 a	VP	VW	HFSL	LO	*Longsight T&RSMD*
08888	E	E	WSWM	BS	*Bescot TMD*
08890	DG	E	WSSE	OC	*Willesden Euroterminal*
08891	B	P	DFLS	FD	*Allerton T&RSMD*
08892	GN	WA	RFSH	BN	*Bounds Green T&RSMD*
08893	DG	E	WSYX	ZB(S)	
08894	B	E	WSXX	AN(S)	
08896	E	E	WSWS	EH	*Avonmouth Bulk Terminal*
08897	E	E	WSWM	BS	*Crewe Diesel TMD*
08899	MM	MA	HISE	DY	*Etches Park T&RSMD*
08900	DG	E	WSWS	EH	*Wabtec, Doncaster*
08901	B	E	WSYX	ZB(S)	
08902	B	EF	WSXX	AN(S)	
08903	EN	EN	MBDL	BG	*ICI, Billingham*
08904	B	E	WSWS	EH	*Did.c.ot Yard*
08905	B	EF	WSWM	BS	*Saltley SD*
08906	B	E	WSXX	ML(S)	
08907	LW	EF	WSWM	BS	*Crewe Diesel TMD*
08908	MM	MA	HISL	NL	*Leeds Neville Hill (InterCity) T&RSMD*
08909	ML	E	WSNW	AN	*Allerton T&RSMD*
08910	B	E	WSSC	ML	*Millerhill Yard*
08911	DG	E	WSNE	TE	*Tees Yard*
08912	B	E	WSNW	AN	*Carlisle Kingmoor Yard*
08913	DG	EF	WSSE	OC	*Stratford SD*

08914	**B**	E	WSXX	ZB(S)	
08915	**F**	E	WSNW	AN	*Warrington Yards*
08918	**DG**	E	WSSE	OC	*Willesden Brent Sidings*
08919	**RX**	E	WSSE	OC	*Temple Mills Yard*
08920	**F**	E	WSWM	BS	*Oxley CARMD*
08921 †	**E**	E	WSAW	CF	*Cardiff Canton TMD*
08922	**DG**	E	WSNW	AN	*Carlisle Kingmoor Yard*
08924	**DG**	E	WSXX	ZB(S)	
08925	**B**	E	WSWX	AN(S)	
08926	**DG**	EF	WSXX	AN(S)	
08927	**B**	E	WSYH	IM	*Immingham TMD*
08928	**0**	AR	HSSN	NC(S)	
08931	**B**	E	WSYX	ZB(S)	
08932	**B**	E	WSXX	CD(S)	
08933	**E**	E	WSSC	ML	*Polmadie T&RSMD*
08934 a	**VP**	VW	HFSN	WN	*Willesden TMD*
08939	**B**	EF	WSWM	BS	*Wabtec, Doncaster*
08940	**B**	E	WSYX	AN(S)	
08941	**B**	E	WSWS	EH	*Fowey Docks*
08942	**B**	E	WSXX	ZB(S)	
08946	**FE**	EF	WSWM	BS	*Dee Marsh Sidings*
08947	**B**	E	WSWS	EH	*Eastleigh Yards*
08948 c	**EP**	EU	GPSS	OC	*North Pole International T&RSMD*
08950	**IM**	MA	HISL	NL(S)	
08951 †	**DG**	EF	WSAW	CF	*Allied Steel & Wire Cardiff*
08953	**DG**	E	WSWS	EH	*St. Blazey T&RSMD*
08954	**T**	E	WSYH	IM	*York Up Yard*
08955	**T**	E	WSXX	CF(S)	
08956	**B**	SO	CDJD	DY	*Serco Railtest, Derby*
08957	**E**	E	WSAW	CF	*Cardiff Docks*
08958	**B**	E	WSXX	SF(S)	

Class 08/9. Reduced height cab. Details as Class 08/0 except:

Converted: 1985–87 by BR at Landore TMD.
Dimensions: 8.92 x 2.59 x 3.60 m.

08993	**E**	E	WSSW	CF	*Margam*
08994 a	**E**	E	WSSW	CF	*Port Talbot Steel Works*
08995 a	**E**	E	WSSW	CF	*Margam*

Names:

08578	Lybert Dickinson	08874	Catherine
08629	BRML WOLVERTON LEVEL 5	08879	Sheffield Childrens Hospital
08649	G.H. Stratton	08896	STEPHEN DENT
08682	Lionheart	08903	John W Antill
08694	PAT BARR	08919	Steep Holm
08701	The Sorter	08950	Neville Hill 1st
08714	Cambridge	08993	ASHBURNHAM
08743	Bryan Turner	08994	GWENDRAETH
08790	M.A. SMITH	08995	KIDWELLY
08869	THE CANARY		

CLASS 09   BR/ENGLISH ELECTRIC   0–6–0

Built: 1959–62 by BR at Darlington or Horwich Works.
Engine: English Electric 6KT of 298 kW (400 h.p.) at 680 r.p.m.
Main Generator: English Electric 801.
Traction Motors: English Electric 506.
Maximum Tractive Effort: 111 kN (25000 lbf).
Continuous Tractive Effort: 39 kN (8800 lbf) at 11.6 m.p.h.
Power At Rail: 201 kW (269 h.p.).   **Train Brakes:** Air & vacuum.
Brake Force: 19 t.   **Dimensions:** 8.92 x 2.59 x 3.89 m.
Weight: 50 t.   **Wheel Diameter:** 1372 mm.
Design Speed: 27 m.p.h.   **Maximum Speed:** 27 m.p.h.
Fuel Capacity: 3037 litres.   **RA:** 5.
Train Supply: Not equipped.   **Multiple Working:** Not equipped.

Class 09/0. Standard Design.

09001	**E**	E	WSWS	EH	*St. Blazey T&RSMD*
09003	**E**	E	WSSW	CF	*Margam*
09004	**B**	SC	HWXX	SU(S)	
09005	**DG**	E	WSYH	IM	*Ferrybridge T&RSMD*
09006	**ML**	E	WSSE	OC	*Hither Green TMD*
09007	**ML**	E	WSYH	IM	*Doncaster TMD*
09008	**E**	E	WSWS	EH	*Tavistock Junction*
09009	**E**	E	WSSE	OC	*Parkeston Yard*
09010	**DG**	E	WSSE	OC	*Wembley Yards*
09011	**DG**	EF	WSWM	BS	*Bescot TMD*
09012	**DG**	E	WSSE	OC	*Hoo Junction*
09013	**DG**	E	WSSW	CF	*Swansea Burrows Sidings*
09014	**DG**	E	WSYH	IM	*Hull King George Dock*
09015	**DG**	E	WSSW	CF	*Sudbrook Pumping Station*
09016	**DG**	E	WSWS	EH	*Tavistock Junction*
09017	**E**	E	WSSW	CF	*Sudbrook Pumping Station*
09018	**E**	E	WSSE	OC	*Wembley Yards*
09019	**ML**	E	WSSE	OC	*Hoo Junction*
09020	**B**	E	WSXX	ZB(S)	
09021	**E**	EF	WSWM	BS	*Bescot TMD*
09022	**E**	EF	WSNW	AN	*Garston Yard*
09023	**E**	E	WSNE	TE	*Tyne Yard SD*
09024	**ML**	E	WSSE	OC	*Hither Green TMD*
09025	**CX**	SC	HWSU	BI	*Brighton T&RSMD*
09026	**G**	SC	HWSU	BI	*Brighton T&RSMD*

Names:

09009 Three Bridges C.E.D	09026 William Pearson
09012 Dick Hardy	

**Class 09/1. Converted from Class 08/0. 110 V electrical equipment. Details
as Class 09/0 except:**

Built: 1960–61 by BR at Crewe, Derby or Horwich Works. Converted 1992–93
by RFS Industries, Kilnhurst.

09101	**DG**	E	WSWS	EH	*Swindon Cocklebury Yard*
09102	**DG**	E	WSSW	CF	*Cardiff Canton TMD*
09103	**DG**	E	WSWM	BS	*Rugby Up Sidings*
09104	**DG**	E	WSSC	ML	*Motherwell T&RSMD*
09105	**DG**	E	WSSW	CF	*Newport Alexandra Dock Junction*
09106	**DG**	E	WSNE	TE	*Tees Yard*
09107	**DG**	E	WSSW	CF	*Newport Alexandra Dock Junction*

Class 09/2. Converted from Class 08/0. 90 V electrical equipment.
Details as Class 09/0 except:

Built: 1958–60 by BR at Crewe or Derby Works. Converted 1992 by RFS Industries, Kilnhurst.

09201 a	**DG**	E	WSYH	IM	*Knottingley T&RSMD*
09202	**DG**	E	WSYH	IM	*Goole Yard*
09203	**DG**	E	WSSW	CF	*Aberthaw*
09204	**DG**	E	WSNE	TE	*Tyne Yard*
09205	**DG**	E	WSSC	ML	*Millerhill Yard*

CLASS 20   ENGLISH ELECTRIC   Bo–Bo

Built: 1957–68 by English Electric Company at Vulcan Foundry, Newton le Willows or by Robert Stephenson & Hawthorn at Darlington.
Engine: English Electric 8SVT Mk. II of 746 kW (1000 h.p.) at 850 r.p.m.
Main Generator: English Electric 819/3C.
Traction Motors: English Electric 526/5D or 526/8D.
Maximum Tractive Effort: 187 kN (42000 lbf).
Continuous Tractive Effort: 111 kN (25000 lbf) at 11 m.p.h.

Power At Rail: 574 kW (770 h.p.).	**Train Brakes:** Air & vacuum.
Brake Force: 35 t.	**Dimensions:** 14.25 x 2.67 x 3.86 m.
Weight: 73.4–73.5 t.	**Wheel Diameter:** 1092 mm.
Design Speed: 75m.p.h.	**Maximum Speed:** 60 m.p.h.
Fuel Capacity: 1727 litres.	**RA:** 5.
Train Supply: Not equipped.	**Multiple Working:** Blue Star.

Class 20/0. Standard Design.

| 20189 | **G** | RT | MBDL | CP | |

Class 20/3. Direct Rail Services refurbished locos. Details as Class 20/0 except:

Refurbished: 1995–96 by Brush Traction at Loughborough (20301–305) or 1997–98 by RFS(E) at Doncaster (20306–315).
Train Brakes: Air.   **Maximum Speed:** 75 m.p.h.
Brake Force: 31 t.   **Fuel Capacity:** 2900 (+ 4909) litres.
Multiple Working: Blue Star (20301–305 at nose end only).

20301	+	**DR**	DR	XHSD	KD	Max Joule 1958–1999
20302		**DR**	DR	XHSD	KD	
20303	+	**DR**	DR	XHSD	KD	
20304		**DR**	DR	XHSD	KD	
20305		**DR**	DR	XHSD	KD	

20306	+	**DR**	DR	XHSD	KD
20307	+	**DR**	DR	XHSD	KD
20308	+	**DR**	DR	XHSD	KD
20309	+	**DR**	DR	XHSD	KD
20310	+	**DR**	DR	XHSD	KD
20311	+	**DR**	DR	XHSD	KD
20312	+	**DR**	DR	XHSD	KD
20313	+	**DR**	DR	XHSD	KD
20314	+	**DR**	DR	XHSD	KD
20315	+	**DR**	DR	XHSD	KD

Class 20/9. Direct Rail Services (former Hunslet-Barclay) refurbished locos.
Details as Class 20/0 except:

Refurbished: 1989 by Hunslet-Barclay at Kilmarnock.
Train Brakes: Air.   **Fuel Capacity:** 1727 (+ 4727) litres.

20901		**DR**	DR	XHSD	KD
20902	+	**DR**	DR	XHSD	KD
20903	+	**DR**	DR	XHSD	KD
20904		**DR**	DR	XHSD	KD
20905	+	**HB**	DR	XHSS	KD(S)
20906		**DR**	DR	XHSD	KD

CLASS 25   BR/BEYER PEACOCK/SULZER   Bo–Bo

Built: 1965 by Beyer Peacock at Gorton.
Engine: Sulzer 6LDA28-B of 930 kW (1250 h.p.) at 750 r.p.m.
Main Generator: AEI RTB15656.   **Traction Motors:** AEI 253AY.
Maximum Tractive Effort: 200 kN (45000 lbf).
Cont. TE: 93 kN (20800 lbf) at 17.1 m.p.h.
Power At Rail: 708 kW (949 h.p.).   **Train Brakes:** Air & vacuum.
Brake Force: 38 t.   **Dimensions:** 15.39 x 2.73 x 3.86 m.
Weight: 71.45 t.   **Wheel Diameter:** 1143 mm.
Design Speed: 90 m.p.h.   **Maximum Speed:** 60 m.p.h.
Fuel Capacity: 2270 litres.   **RA:** 5.
Train Supply: Not equipped.   **Multiple Working:** Blue Star.

Class 25/3. GEC Series 3 Control Equipment.

| 25278 | **GG** | NY | MBDL | NY | SYBILIA |

CLASS 31   BRUSH/ENGLISH ELECTRIC   A1A–A1A

Built: 1958–62 by Brush Traction at Loughborough.
Engine: English Electric 12SVT of 1100 kW (1470 h.p.) at 850 r.p.m.
Main Generator: Brush TG160-48.   **Traction Motors:** Brush TM73-68.
Maximum Tractive Effort: 160 kN (35900 lbf).
Cont. TE: 83 kN (18700 lbf) at 23.5 m.p.h.
Power At Rail: 872 kW (1170 h.p.).   **Train Brakes:** Air & vacuum.
Brake Force: 49 t.   **Dimensions:** 17.30 x 2.67 x 3.87 m.
Weight: 106.7–111 t.   **Wheel Diameter:** 1092/1003 mm.
Design Speed: 90 m.p.h.   **Maximum Speed:** 60 m.p.h.

Fuel Capacity: 2409 litres.   **RA:** 5 or 6.
Train Supply: Not equipped.   **Multiple Working:** Blue Star.
Non-standard numbering:
• 31110 carries number D5528.

Class 31/1. Standard Design. RA: 5.

31110	**G**	E	WMAC	OC	TRACTION magazine
31113	**CE**	E	WNXX	OM(S)	
31119	**CE**	E	WNYX	CL(S)	
31144	**CE**	E	WNYX	CL(S)	
31154	**CE**	E	WNYX	OM(S)	
31190	**FR**	PO	SDFR	TM	GRYPHON
31203	**CE**	E	WNXX	OM(S)	
31207	**CE**	E	WMAC	OC	
31233	**CE**	E	WNYX	OM(S)	Severn Valley Railway
31285	**CE**	E	WNYX	CL(S)	
31306	**CE**	E	WNXX	OM(S)	
31308	**CE**	E	WNXX	OM(S)	
31327	**FQ**	E	WNYX	CL(S)	

Class 31/4. Electric Train Supply equipment. Details as Class 31/1 except:

Maximum Speed: 90 m.p.h.   **RA:** 6.
Train Supply: Electric, but not operational (e – Electric, index 66).

31420 e	**IM**	E	WMAC	OC	
31427	**B**	E	WNXX	SF(S)	
31434	**B**	E	WNXX	HM(S)	
31452 e	**FR**	FR	SDFR	TM	MINOTAUR
31459 e	**FR**	FR	SDFR	TM	CERBERUS
31460	**B**	E	WNYX	BS(S)	
31465	**RR**	E	WNXX	OM(S)	
31466 ae	**E**	E	WMAC	OC	
31468 e	**FR**	FR	SDFR	TM	HYDRA

Class 31/1 ("31/5"). Electric Train Supply equipment fitted, but isolated.
Details as Class 31/1 except:

RA: 6.   **Maximum Speed:** 60 m.p.h.
Train Supply: Electric, isolated.

31512	**CE**	E	WNYX	BS(S)	
31514	**CE**	E	WNXX	OM(S)	
31530	**CE**	E	WNXX	SP(S)	
31533	**CE**	E	WNYX	BS(S)	
31538	**B**	E	WNYX	CL(S)	
31554	**CE**	E	WNXX	WA(S)	
31556	**CE**	E	WNYX	CL(S)	

Class 31/6. Electric Train Supply through wiring and controls. Details as
Class 31/1 except:

Maximum Speed: 90 m.p.h.   **Train Supply:** Electric through wired.

31601	**FR**	FR	SDFR	TM	BLETCHLEY PARK 'STATION X'
31602	**FR**	FR	SDFR	TM	CHIMAERA

CLASS 33   BRCW/SULZER   Bo–Bo

Built: 1960–62 by the Birmingham Railway Carriage & Wagon Company at Smethwick.
Engine: Sulzer 8LDA28 of 1160 kW (1550 h.p.) at 750 r.p.m.
Main Generator: Crompton Parkinson CG391B1.
Traction Motors: Crompton Parkinson C171C2.
Maximum Tractive Effort: 200 kN (45000 lbf).
Continuous Tractive Effort: 116 kN (26000 lbf) at 17.5 m.p.h.
Power At Rail: 906 kW (1215 h.p.).   **Train Brakes:** Air & vacuum.
Brake Force: 35 t.   **Dimensions:** 15.47 x 2.82 x 3.86 m.
Weight: 77.7 t.   **Wheel Diameter:** 1092 mm.
Design Speed: 85 m.p.h.   **Maximum Speed:** 60 (* 75, † 85) m.p.h.
Fuel Capacity: 3410 litres.   **RA:** 6.
Train Supply: Electric, not operational (e – index 48 (750 V d.c. only).
Multiple Working: Blue Star.
Non-standard livery/numbering:

- 33051 also carries number 6569.
- 33109 also carries number D6525.
- 33116 also carries number D6535.
- 33208 carries number D6593.

Class 33/0. Standard Design.

33019	**CE**	E	WNYX	ML(S)	
33021 e†	**R**	WF	SDFR	TM	Eastleigh
33025 *	**CE**	E	WSAC	ML	
33026	**CE**	E	WNYX	EH(S)	
33030 *	**E**	E	WSAC	ML	
33046	**CE**	E	WNYX	EH(S)	
33051	**B**	E	WNYX	EH(S)	Shakespeare Cliff

Class 33/1. Blue Star & BR Southern Region Multiple Working Equipment.
Details as Class 33/0 except:

Train Brakes: Air, vacuum & electro-pneumatic.
Weight: 78.5 t.   **Multiple Working:** Blue Star & SR System.

33103 be†	**G**	CM	CTLO	TM	
33109 be†	**B**	HL	MBDL	RL	Captain Bill Smith RNR
33116 b	**B**	E	WNXX	OC(S)	

Class 33/2. Narrow body profile. Details as Class 33/0 except:

Weight: 77.5 t.   **Dimensions:** 15.47 x 2.64 x 3.86 m.

33202	**CE**	E	WNXX	EH(S)	
33208 e*	**G**	HL	MBDL	RL	

CLASS 37   ENGLISH ELECTRIC   Co–Co

Built: 1960–65 by English Electric Company at Vulcan Foundry, Newton le Willows or by Robert Stephenson & Hawthorn at Darlington.

Engine: English Electric 12CSVT of 1300 kW (1750 h.p.) at 850 r.p.m.
Main Generator: English Electric 822/10G.
Traction Motors: English Electric 538/A.
Maximum Tractive Effort: 245 kN (55500 lbf).
Continuous Tractive Effort: 156 kN (35000 lbf) at 13.6 m.p.h.
Power At Rail: 932 kW (1250 h.p.).   **Train Brakes:** Air & vacuum.
Brake Force: 50 t.   **Dimensions:** 18.75 x 2.74 x 3.94 or 3.99 m.
Weight: 102.8–108.4 t.   **Wheel Diameter:** 1092 mm.
Design Speed: 90 m.p.h.   **Maximum Speed:** 80 m.p.h.
Fuel Capacity: 4046 (+ 7678) litres.   **RA:** 5 (§ 6).
Train Supply: Not equipped.   **Multiple Working:** Blue Star.

Notes: 37073/074/131–308/358/370–383 have roof mounted horns and are 3.99 m. high. The remainder have nose mounted horns and are 3.94 m. high.

Non-standard liveries/numbering:

* 37116 is as **B**, but with Transrail markings.
* 37131 also carries number 6831.
* 37351 carries number 37002 on one side only.
* 37403 carries number D6607.

Class 37/0. Standard Design. Details as above.

37010	a	**CE**	E	WNYX	SP(S)
37013	+	**ML**	E	WNYX	SF(S)
37023		**ML**	E	WNXX	OC(S)	Stratford TMD
						Quality Approved
37029		**B**	RV	RTLO	CP
37037	a	**F**	E	WNYX	SP(S)
37038		**CE**	IR	MBDL	BQ
37040		**E**	E	WNXX	SP(S)
37042	+	**E**	E	WKAC	OC
37046	a	**CE**	E	WNXX	TY(S)
37047	+	**ML**	E	WKAC	OC
37051		**E**	E	WKAC	OC	Merehead
37054		**CE**	E	WNYX	ML(S)
37055	+	**ML**	E	WKAD	CD
37057	+	**E**	E	WKAD	CD	Viking
37058	a+	**CE**	E	WNXX	TY(S)
37059	a+	**FD**	E	WNYX	IM(S)
37065	+	**ML**	E	WKAC	OC
37069	a+	**CE**	E	WNYX	SP(S)
37071	a+	**CE**	E	WNYX	SP(S)
37073	a+	**T**	E	WNYX	SP(S)
37074	a+	**ML**	E	WNYX	SP(S)
37077	a	**ML**	E	WNXX	TY(S)
37087		**CE**	E	WNYX	CW(S)

37097		CE	E	WNYX	MH(S)	
37100	a	T	E	WNXX	TY(S)	
37109		E	E	WKAD	CD	
37114	r+	E	E	WKAD	CD	City of Worcester
37116	+	O	E	WKAD	CD	Sister Dora
37131	+	F	E	WNYX	SP(S)	
37133	a	CE	E	WNYX	SP(S)	
37146	a	CE	E	WNXX	TY(S)	
37152		IS	E	WNYX	ML(S)	
37162	+	DG	E	WNYX	SP(S)	
37165	a+	TC	E	WNYX	TT(S)	
37170	a	TC	E	WNYX	SP(S)	
37174	a	E	E	WKAC	OC	
37175	a	O	E	WNYX	OM(S)	
37178	+	F	E	WNYX	EH(S)	
37185	+	CE	E	WNYX	CF(S)	
37196	a	CE	E	WNXX	TY(S)	
37198	+	ML	E	WNXX	TT(S)	
37203		ML	E	WKAC	OC	
37211		CE	E	WNYX	TE(S)	
37212	+	T	E	WNYX	EH(S)	
37216	+	ML	E	WKAD	CD	
37217	+	B	E	WNYX	AY(S)	
37219		ML	E	WKAC	OC	
37220	+	E	E	WNXX	TT(S)	
37221	a	T	E	WNXX	TY(S)	
37225	+	F	E	WNYX	CF(S)	
37230	+	TC	E	WNXX	TT(S)	
37238	a+	F	E	WNXX	TY(S)	
37248	+	ML	E	WKAC	OC	Midland Railway Centre
37250	a+	T	E	WNXX	TY(S)	
37252		FD	E	WNYX	DD(S)	
37261	a+	FD	E	WNYX	OC(S)	
37262	+	DG	E	WNYX	SP(S)	Dounreay[1]
37263		CE	E	WNYX	EH(S)	
37264		CE	E	WNYX	CF(S)	
37275	+	B	E	WNYX	TT(S)	Oor Wullie
37293	a+	ML	E	WNXX	TY(S)	
37294	a+	CE	E	WNXX	TY(S)	
37298	a+	E	E	WNYX	SP(S)	
37308	(37274)	+	B	E	WNXX	EH(S)

Class 37/3. Re-geared (CP7) bogies. Details as Class 37/0 except:

Maximum Tractive Effort: 250 kN (56180 lbf).
Continuous Tractive Effort: 184 kN (41250 lbf) at 11.4 m.p.h.
Design Speed: 80 m.p.h.

Notes: 37334 has standard bogies, but has not officially been reclassified 37/0.

37331		FM	E	WNYX	DD(S)
37334	a+	F	E	WNYX	IM(S)
37341	+	F	E	WNYX	TE(S)

37344	+	**FD**	E	WNYX	IM(S)
37351	+	**TC**	E	WNXX	TE(S)
37358	+	**F**	E	WNYX	IM(S)
37370	a	**E**	E	WNYX	SP(S)
37372		**ML**	E	WKAC	OC
37375	a+	**ML**	E	WKAD	CD
37376	a+	**F**	E	WNYX	SP(S)
37377	+	**CE**	E	WNXX	EH(S)
37379	a	**ML**	E	WKAC	OC	Ipswich WRD Quality Approved
37383	+	**ML**	E	WNYX	IM(S)

Class 37/4. Refurbished with train supply equipment. Main generator replaced by alternator. Re-geared (CP7) bogies. Details as class 37/0 except:

Main Alternator: Brush BA1005A.   **Power At Rail:** 935 kW (1254 h.p.).
Maximum Tractive Effort: 256 kN (57440 lbf).
Continuous Tractive Effort: 184 kN (41250 lbf) at 11.4 m.p.h.
Dimensions: 18.75 x 2.74 x 3.99 m.   **Weight:** 107 t.
Design Speed: 80 m.p.h.
Fuel Capacity: 7678 (z 4046) litres.   **Train Supply:** Electric, index 38.

37401	**E**	E	WKCD	CD	Mary Queen of Scots
37402	**F**	E	WNXX	CD(S)	Bont Y Bermo
37403	ar **G**	E	WNXX	CF(S)	Ben Cruachan
37405	r **E**	E	WKBM	ML	
37406	**T**	E	WNXX	CF(S)	The Saltire Society
37407	**T**	E	WNXX	CD(S)	Blackpool Tower
37408	r **E**	E	WKBM	ML	Loch Rannoch
37409	r **T**	E	WNXX	ML(S)	Loch Awe
37410	**T**	E	WNXX	ML(S)	Aluminium 100
37411	r **E**	E	WKBM	ML	Ty Hafan
37412	**T**	E	WKCD	CD	Driver John Elliott
37413	r **E**	E	WKCD	CD	
37414	**RR**	E	WNXX	CF(S)	Cathays C & W Works 1846–1993
37415	r **E**	E	WKBM	ML	
37416	r **E**	E	WKBM	ML	
37417	a **E**	E	WNXX	BW(S)	
37418	r **E**	E	WKBM	ML	East Lancashire Railway
37419	r **E**	E	WKBM	ML	
37420	**RR**	E	WNXX	CD(S)	The Scottish Hosteller
37421	**E**	E	WKCD	CD	
37422	**RR**	E	WNXX	BW(S)	
37423	**T**	E	WNXX	ML(S)	Sir Murray Morrison 1873-1948 Pioneer of the British Aluminium Industry
37424	**T**	E	WNXX	ML(S)	
37425	**RR**	E	WNXX	CF(S)	Sir Robert McAlpine/Concrete Bob
37426	**E**	E	WKCD	CD	
37427	r **E**	E	WKBM	ML	
37428	r **GS**	E	WKBM	ML	
37429	**RR**	E	WKCD	CD	Eisteddfod Genedlaethol
37430	ar **T**	E	WNXX	ML(S)	Cwmbrân

Class 37/5. Refurbished without train supply equipment. Main generator replaced by alternator. Re-geared (CP7) bogies. Details as Class 37/4 except:

Maximum Tractive Effort: 248 kN (55590 lbf).
Dimensions: 18.75 x 2.74 x 3.94 or 3.99 m.
Weight: 106.1–107.3 (§ 110.0) t.   **Train Supply:** Not equipped.

Notes: 37610–679/682–698/800–899 have roof mounted horns and are 3.99 m. high. The remainder have nose mounted horns and are 3.94 m. high.

37503	r§	**E**	E	WKSN	TO
37505	a§	**T**	E	WKSN	TO
37509	a§	**F**	E	WKSN	TO
37510	a	**IS**	E	WNXX	TE(S)
37513	as§	**LH**	E	WKSN	TO
37515	as	**FM**	E	WNXX	TE(S)
37516	s§	**LH**	E	WKSN	TO
37517	ass§	**LH**	E	WKSN	TO
37518	a§	**FM**	E	WKSN	TO
37519		**FM**	E	WNYX	EH(S)
37520	r§	**E**	E	WKSN	TO
37521	r§	**E**	E	WKSN	TO

British Steel Workington (aligned with 37503–37509)

English China Clays (aligned with 37521)

Class 37/6. Refurbished for Nightstar services. Main generator replaced by alternator, re-geared bogies and UIC jumpers. Details as class 37/5 except:

Maximum Speed: 80 († 90) m.p.h.   **Train Brake:** Air.
Train Supply: Not equipped, but electric through wired.
Multiple Working: TDM († plus Blue Star).

Note: One (unspecified) locomotive is hired from Eurostar (UK) to Freightliner for use on the West Highland Line (Craigendoran Junction–Fort William). This locomotive is outbased at Motherwell T&RSMD.

37601		**EP**	EU	GPSV	OC
37602		**EP**	EU	GPSV	OC
37603		**EP**	EU	GPSV	OC
37604		**EP**	EU	GPSV	OC
37605		**EP**	EU	GPSV	OC
37606		**EP**	EU	GPSV	OC
37607	†	**DR**	DR	XHSD	KD
37608	†	**DR**	DR	XHSD	KD
37609	†	**DR**	DR	XHSD	KD
37610	†	**DR**	DR	XHSD	KD
37611	†	**DR**	DR	XHSD	KD
37612	†	**DR**	DR	XHSD	KD

Class 37/5 (Continued).

37667	rs§	**E**	E	WKSN	TO
37668	s§	**E**	E	WKSN	TO
37669	r§	**E**	E	WKSN	TO
37670	r§	**E**	E	WKSN	TO
37671	a	**T**	E	WNXX	TY(S)
37672	as	**T**	E	WNXX	TE(S)
37673	§	**T**	E	WKSN	TO

Meldon Quarry Centenary (aligned with 37667–37670)

37674 §	**T**	E	WKSN	TO	St. Blaise Church 1445–1995
37675 as§	**T**	E	WKSN	TO	
37676 a§	**F**	E	WKSN	TO	
37677 a§	**F**	E	WKSN	TO	
37678 a§	**F**	E	WKSN	TO	
37679 a§	**F**	E	WKSN	TO	
37680 a§	**FA**	E	WKSN	TO	
37682 r§	**E**	E	WKSN	TO	Hartlepool Pipe Mill
37683 a	**T**	E	WNXX	TE(S)	
37684 ar§	**E**	E	WKSN	TO	Peak National Park
37685 a§	**IS**	E	WKSN	TO	
37686 a	**FA**	E	WNYX	SP(S)	
37688 §	**E**	E	WKSN	TO	
37689 a§	**F**	E	WKSN	TO	
37692	**FC**	E	WKSN	TO	The Lass O' Ballochmyle
37693 as	**T**	E	WNXX	TY(S)	
37694 §	**E**	E	WKSN	TO	
37695 s§	**E**	E	WKSN	TO	
37696 as	**T**	E	WNXX	TY(S)	
37697 §	**E**	E	WNXX	TY(S)	
37698 s§	**LH**	E	WKSN	TO	

Class 37/7. Refurbished locos. Main generator replaced by alternator. Re-geared (CP7) bogies. Ballast weights added. Details as class 37/5 except:
Main Alternator: GEC G564AZ (37796–803) Brush BA1005A (others).
Maximum Tractive Effort: 276 kN   (62000 lbf).
Weight: 120 t.   **RA:** 7.

37701 as	**T**	E	WNXX	OM(S)	
37702 s	**T**	E	WKAD	CD	Taff Merthyr
37703	**T**	E	WKGS	TE(S)	
37704 s	**E**	E	WKAD	CD	
37705	**MG**	E	WNXX	ML(S)	
37706	**E**	E	WKAD	CD	
37707	**E**	E	WKAD	CD	
37708 a	**FP**	E	WNXX	TY(S)	
37709	**MG**	E	WNXX	IM(S)	
37710	**LH**	E	WKAD	CD	
37711	**FM**	E	WNYX	TO(S)	
37712 a	**E**	E	WKAC	OC	
37713	**LH**	E	WNXX	CD(S)	
37714 a	**E**	E	WKGS	TO(S)	
37715	**MG**	E	WNYX	SP(S)	
37716	**E**	E	WKGS	EH(S)	
37717	**E**	E	WKAD	CD	Berwick Middle School, Railsafe Trophy Winners 1998
37718	**E**	E	WKGS	TO(S)	
37719 a	**FP**	E	WNXX	OM(S)	
37796 as	**FC**	E	WNXX	TY(S)	
37797 s	**E**	E	WKAD	CD	
37798	**ML**	E	WKAD	CD	
37799 as	**T**	E	WKAD	CD	Sir Dyfed/County of Dyfed

37800 a	MG	E	WNXX	TY(S)	
37801 s	E	E	WKAD	CD	
37802 s	T	E	WNXX	OM(S)	
37803 a	ML	E	WNXX	TY(S)	
37883	E	E	WKGS	CD(S)	
37884	LH	E	WKAD		Gartcosh
37885	E	E	WKGS	EH(S)	
37886	E	E	WKAD	CD	
37887 s	T	E	WNXX	IM(S)	
37888 z	F	E	WNXX	TE(S)	
37889	T	E	WNYX	CD(S)	
37890 a	MG	E	WNXX	TY(S)	
37891 a	MG	E	WNXX	TY(S)	
37892	MG	E	WNXX	OM(S)	Ripple Lane[1]
37893	E	E	WKAD	CD	
37894 as	FC	E	WNXX	TY(S)	
37895 s	E	E	WKAD	CD	
37896 s	T	E	WNXX	TY(S)	
37897 s	T	E	WNXX	BS(S)	
37898 s	T	E	WNXX	CF(S)	Cwmbargoed DP
37899 s	E	E	WKGS	TE(S)	

Class 37/9. Refurbished locos. New power unit. Main generator replaced by alternator. Ballast weights added. Details as Class 37/4 except:

Engine: Mirrlees MB275T of 1340 kW (1800 h.p.) at 1000 r.p.m. (‡ Ruston RK270T of 1340 kW (1800 h.p.) at 900 r.p.m.).   **Train supply:** Not equipped.
Main Alternator: Brush BA1005A (‡ GEC G564AZ).
Maximum Tractive Effort: 279 kN (62680 lbf).
Continuous Tractive Effort: 184 kN (41250 lbf) at 11.4 m.p.h.
Weight: 120 t.   **RA:** 7.

37901	T	E	WNYX	CF(S)	Mirrlees Pioneer
37902	FM	E	WNYX	IM(S)	
37903	FM	E	WNYX	CD(S)	
37905 ‡s	FM	E	WNYX	IM(S)	
37906 ‡s	FO	E	WNYX	KR(S)	

CLASS 43   BREL/PAXMAN   Bo–Bo

Built: 1976–82 by BREL at Crewe Works.
Engine: Paxman Valenta 12RP200L of 1680 kW (2250 h.p.) at 1500 r.p.m. († Paxman 12VP185 of 2010 kW (2700 h.p.) at 1800 r.p.m.).
Main Alternator: Brush BA1001B.
Traction Motors: Brush TMH68–46 or GEC G417AZ, frame mounted.
Maximum Tractive Effort: 80 kN (17980 lbf).
Continuous Tractive Effort: 46 kN (10340 lbf) at 64.5 m.p.h.
Power At Rail: 1320 kW (1770 h.p.).   **Train Brakes:** Air.
Brake Force: 35 t.   **Dimensions:** 17.79 x 2.71 x 3.88 m.
Weight: 70 t.   **Wheel Diameter:** 1020 mm.
Design Speed: 125 m.p.h.   **Maximum Speed:** 125 m.p.h.

Fuel Capacity: 4500 litres. **RA:** 5.
Train Supply: Three-phase electric.
Multiple Working: Within class, jumpers at non-driving end only.

43002	FG	A	IWRP	PM	Techni?uest
43003	FG	A	IWRP	PM	
43004	FG	A	IWRP	PM	Borough of Swindon
43005	FG	A	IWRP	PM	
43006	IS	A	IWCP	LA	
43007	IS	A	IWCP	LA	
43008	V	A	IWCP	LA	
43009	FG	A	IWRP	PM	
43010	FG	A	IWRP	PM	
43011	FG	A	SCXL	ZC(S)	Reader 125
43012	FG	A	IWRP	PM	
43013	V	P	ICCP	LA	
43014	V	P	ICCP	LA	
43015	FG	A	IWRP	PM	
43016	FG	A	IWRP	PM	
43017	FG	A	IWRP	LA	
43018	FG	A	IWRP	LA	The Red Cross
43019	FG	A	IWRP	LA	Dinas Abertawe/City of Swansea
43020	FG	A	IWRP	LA	John Grooms
43021	FG	A	IWRP	LA	
43022	FG	A	IWRP	LA	
43023	FG	A	IWRP	LA	County of Cornwall
43024	FG	A	IWRP	LA	
43025	FG	A	IWRP	LA	Exeter
43026	FG	A	IWRP	LA	City of Westminster
43027	FG	A	IWRP	LA	Glorious Devon
43028	FG	A	IWRP	LA	
43029	IS	A	ICCP	LA	
43030	FG	A	IWRP	PM	Christian Lewis Trust
43031	FG	A	IWRP	PM	
43032	FG	A	IWRP	PM	The Royal Regiment of Wales
43033	FG	A	IWRP	PM	
43034	FG	A	IWRP	PM	The Black Horse
43035	FG	A	IWRP	PM	
43036	FG	A	IWRP	PM	
43037	FG	A	IWRP	PM	
43038	GN	A	IECP	EC	
43039	GN	A	IECP	EC	
43040	FG	A	IWRP	PM	
43041	FG	A	IWRP	LA	City of Discovery
43042	FG	A	IWRP	LA	
43043	MM	P	IMLP	NL	LEICESTERSHIRE COUNTY CRICKET CLUB
43044	MM	P	IMLP	NL	Borough of Kettering
43045	MM	P	IMLP	NL	
43046	MM	P	IMLP	NL	Royal Philharmonic
43047 †	MM	P	IMLP	NL	
43048	MM	P	IMLP	NL	

43049	MM	P	IMLP	NL	Neville Hill
43050	MM	P	IMLP	NL	
43051	MM	P	IMLP	NL	
43052	MM	P	IMLP	NL	
43053	MM	P	IMLP	NL	Leeds United
43054	MM	P	IMLP	NL	
43055	MM	P	IMLP	NL	Sheffield Star
43056	MM	P	IMLP	NL	
43057	MM	P	IMLP	NL	
43058	MM	P	IMLP	NL	MIDLAND PRIDE
43059 †	MM	P	IMLP	NL	
43060	MM	P	IMLP	NL	County of Leicestershire
43061	MM	P	IMLP	NL	
43062	V	P	ICCP	LA	
43063	V	P	ICCP	LA	Maiden Voyager
43064	MM	P	IMLP	NL	
43065	V	P	ICCP	LA	
43066	MM	P	IMLP	NL	Nottingham Playhouse
43067	V	P	ICCP	LA	
43068	V	P	ICCP	LA	The Red Arrows
43069	V	P	ICCP	LA	
43070	V	P	ICCP	LA	
43071	V	P	ICCP	LA	Forward Birmingham
43072	MM	P	IMLP	NL	Derby Etches Park
43073	MM	P	IMLP	NL	
43074 †	MM	P	IMLP	NL	BBC EAST MIDLANDS TODAY
43075 †	MM	P	IMLP	NL	
43076	MM	P	IMLP	NL	THE MASTER CUTLER 1947-1997
43077	MM	P	IMLP	NL	
43078	V	P	ICCP	LA	Golowan Festival Penzance
43079	V	P	ICCP	LA	
43080	V	P	ICCP	LA	
43081	MM	P	IMLP	NL	
43082	MM	P	IMLP	NL	DERBYSHIRE FIRST
43083	MM	P	IMLP	NL	
43084	V	P	ICCP	LA	County of Derbyshire
43085	MM	P	IMLP	NL	
43086	V	P	ICCP	LA	
43087	V	P	ICCP	LA	
43088	V	P	ICCP	LA	
43089	V	P	ICCP	LA	
43090	V	P	ICCP	LA	
43091	V	P	ICCP	LA	
43092	V	P	ICCP	LA	Institution of Mechanical Engineers 150th Anniversary
43093	V	P	ICCP	LA	Lady in Red
43094	V	P	ICCP	LA	
43095	GN	A	IECP	EC	
43096	GN	A	IECP	EC	The Great Racer
43097	V	P	ICCP	LA	
43098	V	P	ICCP	LA	railwaychildren

43099	V	P	ICCP	LA	
43100	V	P	ICCP	LA	
43101	V	P	ICCP	LA	
43102	V	P	ICCP	LA	
43103	V	P	ICCP	LA	
43104	IS	A	SCXL	ZC(S)	County of Cleveland
43105	GN	A	IECP	EC	
43106	GN	A	IECP	EC	
43107	GN	A	IECP	EC	
43108	GN	A	IECP	EC	Old Course St Andrews
43109	GN	A	IECP	EC	
43110	GN	A	IECP	EC	
43111	GN	A	IECP	EC	
43112	GN	A	IECP	EC	
43113	GN	A	IECP	EC	
43114	GN	A	IECP	EC	
43115	GN	A	IECP	EC	
43116	GN	A	IECP	EC	
43117	GN	A	IECP	EC	
43118	GN	A	IECP	EC	
43119	GN	A	IECP	EC	
43120	GN	A	IECP	EC	
43121	V	P	ICCP	LA	
43122	V	P	ICCP	LA	South Yorkshire Metropolitan County
43123	V	P	ICCP	LA	
43124	FG	A	IWRP	PM	
43125	FG	A	IWRP	PM	Merchant Venturer
43126	FG	A	IWRP	PM	City of Bristol
43127	FG	A	IWRP	PM	
43128	FG	A	IWRP	PM	
43129	FG	A	IWRP	PM	
43130	FG	A	IWRP	PM	Sulis Minerva
43131	FG	A	IWRP	PM	Sir Felix Pole
43132	FG	A	IWRP	PM	
43133	FG	A	IWRP	PM	
43134	FG	A	IWRP	PM	County of Somerset
43135	FG	A	IWRP	PM	
43136	FG	A	IWRP	PM	
43137	FG	A	IWRP	PM	Newton Abbot 150
43138	FG	A	IWRP	PM	
43139	FG	A	IWRP	PM	
43140	FG	A	IWRP	PM	
43141	FG	A	IWRP	PM	
43142	FG	A	IWRP	PM	
43143	FG	A	IWRP	PM	
43144	FG	A	IWRP	PM	
43145	FG	A	IWRP	PM	
43146	FG	A	IWRP	PM	
43147	FG	A	IWRP	PM	
43148	FG	A	IWRP	PM	
43149	FG	A	IWRP	PM	B.B.C. Wales Today

43150	FG	A	IWRP	PM	Bristol Evening Post
43151	FG	A	IWRP	PM	
43152	FG	A	IWRP	PM	
43153	V	P	ICCP	LA	THE ENGLISH RIVIERA TORQUAY PAIGNTON BRIXHAM
43154	V	P	ICCP	LA	INTERCITY
43155	V	P	ICCP	LA	City of Aberdeen
43156	V	P	ICCP	LA	
43157	V	P	ICCP	LA	
43158	V	P	ICCP	LA	
43159	V	P	ICCP	LA	
43160	V	P	ICCP	LA	
43161	V	P	ICCP	LA	
43162	V	P	ICCP	LA	
43163	FG	A	IWRP	LA	
43164	FG	A	IWRP	LA	
43165	FG	A	IWRP	LA	
43166	IS	A	ICCP	LA	
43167 †	GN	A	IECP	EC	
43168 †	FG	A	IWRP	LA	
43169 †	FG	A	IWRP	LA	The National Trust
43170 †	FG	A	IWRP	LA	Edward Paxman
43171	FG	A	IWRP	LA	
43172	FG	A	IWRP	LA	
43174	FG	A	IWRP	LA	Bristol-Bordeaux
43175 †	FG	A	IWRP	LA	
43176	FG	A	IWRP	LA	
43177 †	FG	A	IWRP	LA	University of Exeter
43178	V	A	IWCP	LA	
43179 †	FG	A	IWRP	LA	Pride of Laira
43180	V	P	ICCP	LA	City of Newcastle upon Tyne
43181	FG	A	IWRP	LA	Devonport Royal Dockyard 1693–1993
43182	FG	A	IWRP	LA	
43183	FG	A	IWRP	LA	
43184	V	A	IWCP	LA	
43185	FG	A	IWRP	LA	Great Western
43186	FG	A	IWRP	LA	Sir Francis Drake
43187	FG	A	IWRP	LA	
43188	FG	A	IWRP	LA	City of Plymouth
43189	FG	A	IWRP	LA	RAILWAY HERITAGE TRUST
43190	FG	A	IWRP	LA	
43191 †	FG	A	IWRP	LA	Seahawk
43192	FG	A	IWRP	LA	City of Truro
43193	V	P	ICCP	LA	Plymouth SPIRIT OF DISCOVERY
43194	V	P	ICCP	LA	
43195	IS	P	ICCP	LA	British Red Cross 125th Birthday 1995¹
43196	V	P	ICCP	LA	The Newspaper Society Founded 1836
43197	V	P	ICCP	LA	Railway Magazine Centenary 1897–1997
43198	V	P	ICCP	LA	HMS Penzance

CLASS 46   BR/SULZER   1Co–Co1

Built: 1963 by BR at Derby Locomotive Works.
Engine: Sulzer 12LDA28B of 1860 kW (2500 h.p.) at 750 r.p.m.
Main Generator: Brush TG160-60.   **Traction Motors:** Brush TM73-68 Mk3.
Maximum Tractive Effort: 245 kN (55000 lbf).
Continuous Tractive Effort: 141 kN (31600 lbf) at 22.3 m.p.h.
Power At Rail: 1460 kW (1960 h.p.).   **Train Brakes:** Air & vacuum.
Brake Force: 63 t.   **Dimensions:** 20.70 x 2.78 x 3.92 m.
Weight: 140 t.   **Wheel Diameter:** 914/1143 mm.
Design Speed: 90 m.p.h.   **Maximum Speed:** 75 m.p.h.
Fuel Capacity: 3591 litres.   **RA:** 7.
Train Supply: Not equipped.   **Multiple Working:** Not equipped.
Non-standard livery/numbering:
• 46035 carries number D172. Official RSL number is 89472.

46035   **G**   CN   MBDL   CQ   Ixion

CLASS 47   BR/BRUSH/SULZER   Co–Co

Built: 1963–67 by Brush Traction, at Loughborough or by BR at Crewe Works.
Engine: Sulzer 12LDA28C of 1920 kW(*‡ 1785 kW) (2580 (*‡2400) h.p.) at 750 r.p.m.
Main Generator: Brush TG160-60 Mk4 or TM172-50 Mk1.
Traction Motors: Brush TM64-68 Mk1 or Mk1A.
Maximum Tractive Effort: 267 kN (60000 lbf).
Continuous Tractive Effort: 133 kN (30000 lbf) at 26 m.p.h.
Power At Rail: 1550 kW (2080 h.p.).   **Train Brakes:** Air.
Brake Force: 61 t.   **Dimensions:** 19.38 x 2.79 x 3.9 m.
Weight: 111.5–120.6 t.   **Wheel Diameter:** 1143 mm.
Design Speed: 95 m.p.h.   **Maximum Speed:** 75 m.p.h.
Fuel Capacity: 3273 (+ 5550; † 4410 litres).
Train Supply: Not equipped.
Multiple Working: Green Circle (n – not equipped).

Notes:
d Dock Mode' slow speed traction control system for working trains from Felixstowe North Container Terminal.

Non-standard liveries/numbering:
• 47004 carries number D1524.
• 47114 is as **GG**, but with Freightliner logos.
• 47145 is dark blue with Railfreight Distribution logos.
• 47515 is livery **IM** on one side and all-over white on the other side).
• 47519 also carries number D1102.

Class 47/0 (Dual braked locos) or Class 47/2 (Air braked locos). Standard Design. Details as above.

47004 xn **GG** E   WNXX   KR(S)

Number	Flags					Notes
47052	*	FF	P	DFLT	FD	
47053	+	FE	EF	WNYX	HM(S)	
47095	+	FE	EF	WNYX	AN(S)	
47114	*+	0	FL	DFLM	FD	Freightlinerbulk
47145	+	0	EF	WNYX	CD(S)	MERDDIN EMRYS
47146	+	FE	EF	WNYX	CD(S)	
47150	*+	FL	FL	DFLM	FD	
47152	*+	FF	FL	DFLM	FD	
47157	*+	FF	P	DFLT	FD	Johnson Stevens Agencies
47186	+	FE	EF	WNYX	HM(S)	
47188	+	FE	EF	WNYX	CD(S)	
47193	n*	FL	P	DHLT	CG(S)	
47197	dn*	FF	P	DFFT	FD	
47200	*+	FE	EF	WNYX	HM(S)	
47201	*+	FE	EF	WNYX	HM(S)	
47205	*+	FF	FL	DFLM	FD	
47206	n*	FF	P	DFLT	FD	The Morris Dancer
47207	*+	FF	P	DFLM	FD	The Felixstowe Partnership
47209	*+	FF	P	DHLT	CG(S)	
47211	+	FD	EF	WNYX	EH(S)	
47212	xn‡	FF	P	DFLT	FD	
47213	+	FD	EF	WNYX	SP(S)	
47217	+	FE	EF	WNYX	SP(S)	
47218	+	FE	EF	WNYX	SP(S)	
47219	+	FE	EF	WNYX	HM(S)	
47221	xn†	FP	E	WNYX	LB(S)	
47224	xn‡	F	P	DFLT	FD	
47225	n*	FF	P	DHLT	CG(S)	
47226	+	FD	EF	WNYX	HM(S)	
47228	+	FE	EF	WNYX	HM(S)	
47229	+	FD	EF	WNYX	HM(S)	
47234	*+	FF	P	DFLM	FD	
47236	+	FE	EF	WNYX	SF(S)	
47237	+	FE	EF	WNYX	HM(S)	
47241	+	FE	EF	WNYX	HM(S)	
47245	+	FE	EF	WNYX	DD(S)	
47256	xn	FD	E	WNYX	DD(S)	
47258	*+	FL	FL	DFLM	FD	Forth Ports Tilbury
47270	dn*	FF	P	DFFT	FD	Cory Brothers 1842–1992
47279	*+	FF	P	DFLM	FD	
47280	+	FD	EF	WNYX	HM(S)	
47283	n*	FF	FL	DHLT	ST(S)	
47285	+	FE	EF	WNYX	TT(S)	
47287	*+	F	FL	DFLM	FD	
47289	*+	FF	P	DFLM	FD	
47290	*+	FF	FL	DHLT	CG(S)	
47292	*+	F	P	DFLM	FD	
47293	+	FE	EF	WNYX	HM(S)	
47295	xdn‡	F	FL	DFFT	FD	
47296	xn*	FF	P	DFLT	FD	
47298	+	FD	EF	WNYX	HM(S)	

Class 47/3 (Dual braked locos) or Class 47/2 (Air braked locos).
Details as Class 47/0 except:

Weight: 113.7 t.

47301 *+	FF	P	DFLM	FD	Freightliner Birmingham
47302 *+	FF	FL	DFLM	FD	
47303 *+	FF	P	DFLM	FD	Freightliner Cleveland
47305 n	FF	P	DHLT	CG(S)	
47306 *+	FF	EF	WNXX	EH(S)	The Sapper
47307 +	FE	EF	WNYX	HM(S)	
47308 *	FF	FL	DHLT	CG(S)	
47309 d*+	FF	FL	DHLT	CD(S)	European Rail Operator of The Year
47310 +	FE	EF	WNYX	HM(S)	
47312 +	FE	EF	WNYX	CD(S)	
47313 +	FD	EF	WNYX	HM(S)	
47314 +	FD	EF	WNYX	HM(S)	
47316 +	FE	EF	WNYX	TT(S)	
47323 d*+	FF	P	DFFT	FD	
47326 +	FE	EF	WNYX	CD(S)	Saltley Depot Quality Approved
47328 +	FD	EF	WNYX	CW(S)	
47330 *+	FF	FL	DHLT	CG(S)	
47331 xns	CE	E	WNYX	SP(S)	
47334 n*	FF	P	DFLT	FD	P & O Nedlloyd
47335 +	FD	EF	WNYX	HM(S)	
47337 *+	FF	FL	DHLT	CG(S)	
47338 +	FE	EF	WNYX	CD(S)	
47339 n*	FF	P	DHLT	CG(S)	
47345 n*	FF	P	DFLT	FD	
47348 +	FE	EF	WNYX	SF(S)	St. Christopher's Railway Home
47349 xn*	FF	P	DFLT	FD	
47353 n*	FF	FL	DHLT	CG(S)	
47354 *	FF	FL	DHLT	CG(S)	
47357 xn	CE	E	WNYX	BS(S)	
47358 *+	FF	P	DFLM	FD	
47360 +	FE	EF	WNYX	HM(S)	
47361 *+	FF	P	DFLM	FD	
47362 +	FD	EF	WNYX	SP(S)	
47365 +	FE	EF	WNYX	CF(S)	Diamond Jubilee
47367 *+	FF	P	DFLM	FD	
47368 xn	F	E	WNYX	SF(S)	
47370 *+	FF	P	DFLM	FD	Andrew A Hodgkinson
47371 n*	FF	P	DHLT	CB(S)	
47372 n*	FF	P	DFLT	FD	
47375 +	FE	EF	WNYX	HM(S)	
47376 xn*	FF	P	DFLT	FD	Freightliner 1995
47377 n*	FF	P	DHLT	CB(S)	

Class 47/4. Electric Train Supply equipment. Details as Class 47/0 except:

Weight: 120.4–125.1 t.
Fuel Capacity: 3273 (+ 5887) litres.
Train Supply: Electric, index 66.

Maximum Speed: 95 (* 75) m.p.h.
RA: 7.

Multiple Working: Not equipped (m – Green Circle; † – Blue Star).

47462 x	RG	E	WNYX	TT(S)	
47471 x	I	E	WNYX	CW(S)	
47474 x	RG	E	WNYX	CD(S)	Sir Rowland Hill
47475 x	RX	E	WNYX	HM(S)	
47476 x	RG	E	WNYX	TT(S)	Night Mail
47478 x	B	E	WNYX	SP(S)	
47481 x	BL	E	WNYX	CW(S)	
47488 x	GG	FR	IANA	TM	
47489	RG	E	WNYX	SP(S)	
47492 x	RX	E	WNYX	OC(S)	
47501 x	RG	E	WNYX	CD(S)	Craftsman¹
47513 x	BL	E	WNYX	CD(S)	
47515 x	O	E	WNYX	CW(S)	
47519 x+	GG	E	WNYX	CD(S)	
47524 x	RX	E	WNYX	CW(S)	
47525 x	FE	E	WNYX	CD(S)	
47526 x	BL	E	WNYX	CW(S)	
47528 x	IM	E	WNYX	DD(S)	
47530 x	RX	E	WNYX	SP(S)	
47532 x	RX	E	WNYX	SP(S)	
47535 x	RX	E	WNYX	OC(S)	
47536 x	RX	E	WNYX	CD(S)	
47539	RX	E	WNYX	ZC(S)	
47540 xm	CE	E	WNYX	CW(S)	The Institution of Civil Engineers
47547	N	E	WNYX	CD(S)	
47550 x	IM	E	WNYX	IM(S)	
47566 x	RX	E	WNYX	SP(S)	
47574 x	RG	E	WNYX	CD(S)	
47575 x	RG	E	WHCD	CD	City of Hereford
47576 x	RX	E	WNYX	CW(S)	
47596 x	RX	E	WNYX	CD(S)	
47624 xj	RX	E	WNYX	AN(S)	
47634	RG	E	WHCD	CD	Holbeck
47635 xj	RG	E	WHCD	CD	
47640 j	RG	E	WNYX	CD(S)	University of Strathclyde

Class 47/7. Electric Train Supply and Push & Pull equipment (RCH System).
Details as Class 47/4 except:

Weight: 118.7 t. **Fuel Capacity:** 5887 litres.

47701 x	FR	WF	SDFR	TM	Waverley
47702 x	V	E	WNYX	TT(S)	County of Suffolk
47703 x	FR	FR	SDFR	TM	HERMES
47705 x	LW	RV	RTLO	CP	GUY FAWKES
47707 x	RX	E	WNYX	CW(S)	Holyrood
47709 x	FR	FR	SDFR	TM	
47710 x	FR	FR	SDFR	TM	
47711 x	V	E	WNYX	TT(S)	County of Hertfordshire
47712 x	WL	FR	SDFR	TM	
47714 x	RX	E	WNYX	CW(S)	

47715	**N**	E	WNYX	CW(S)	
47716 x	**RX**	E	WNYX	CW(S)	
47717 x	**RG**	E	WNYX	CW(S)	

Class 47/7. Electric Train Supply equipment and RCH Jumper Cables. Details as Class 47/4 except:

Weight: 118.7 t.   **Fuel Capacity:** 5887 litres.

47721	**RX**	E	WHCD	CD	Saint Bede
47722	**V**	E	ILRA	TO	The Queen Mother
47725	**RX**	E	WHCD	CD	The Railway Mission
47726	**RX**	E	WHTD	CD	Manchester Airport Progress
47727	**RX**	E	WHCD	CD	Duke of Edinburgh's Award
47732 x	**RX**	E	WHCD	CD	Restormel
47733	**RX**	E	WHTD	CD	Eastern Star
47734	**RX**	E	WHTD	CD	Crewe Diesel Depot Quality Approved
47736	**RX**	E	WHCD	CD	Cambridge Traction & Rolling Stock Depot
47737	**RX**	E	WHCD	CD	Resurgent
47738	**RX**	E	WHCD	CD	Bristol Barton Hill
47739	**RX**	E	WHCD	CD	Resourceful
47741	**RX**	E	ILRA	TO	Resilient
47742	**RX**	E	ILRA	TO	The Enterprising Scot
47744	**E**	E	WHCD	CD	
47745 x	**RX**	E	WNYX	TT(S)	Royal London Society for the Blind
47746	**RX**	E	WHCD	CD	The Bobby
47747	**V**	E	ILRA	TO	Graham Farish
47749	**RX**	E	WHCD	CD	Atlantic College
47750	**V**	E	ILRA	TO	ATLAS
47756	**RX**	E	WHCM	ML	Royal Mail Tyneside
47757	**RX**	E	WHCD	CD	Restitution
47758	**E**	E	WHCD	CD	Regency Rail Cruises
47759	**RX**	E	WHCD	CD	
47760	**E**	E	WHCM	ML	Ribblehead Viaduct
47761	**RX**	E	WHCD	CD	
47762	**RX**	E	WHCD	CD	
47763	**RX**	E	WNXX	ML(S)	
47764	**RX**	E	WHCD	CD	Resounding
47765 x	**RX**	E	WNXX	BK(S)	Ressaldar
47766 x	**RX**	E	WNXX	TT(S)	Resolute
47767	**RX**	E	WHCD	CD	Saint Columba
47768 x	**RX**	E	WNXX	CD(S)	
47769	**V**	E	ILRA	TO	Resolve
47770	**RX**	E	WNXX	CF(S)	Reserved
47771	**RX**	E	WNXX	CD(S)	Heaton Traincare Depot
47772 x	**RX**	E	WHCD	CD	
47773	**RX**	E	WHCM	ML	Reservist
47774 x	**RX**	E	WHCD	CD	Poste Restante
47775 x	**RX**	E	WHTD	CD	Respite
47776 x	**RX**	E	WHCD	CD	Respected

47777 x	**RX**	E	WNXX	TT(S)	Restored
47778	**RX**	E	WHCD	CD	Irresistible
47779	**RX**	E	WNXX	CD(S)	
47780	**RX**	E	WHCD	CD	
47781	**RX**	E	WHCD	CD	Isle of Iona
47782	**RX**	E	WNXX	CF(S)	
47783	**RX**	E	WHCD	CD	Saint Peter
47784	**RX**	E	WHCD	CD	Condover Hall
47785	**E**	E	WHCD	CD	Fiona Castle
47786	**E**	E	WHCD	CD	Roy Castle OBE
47787	**RX**	E	WHCD	CD	Victim Support
47789	**RX**	E	WHCD	CD	Lindisfarne
47790	**RX**	E	WHCM	ML	Dewi Sant/Saint David
47791	**RX**	E	WHCM	ML	
47792	**RX**	E	WHCD	CD	Saint Cuthbert
47793	**RX**	E	WHCD	CD	Saint Augustine

Class 47/7. Electric Train Supply equipment. Locos dedicated for Royal Train & (occasional) Charter Train use. Details as Class 47/4 except:

Weight: 118.7 t.   **Fuel Capacity:** 5887 litres.

47798	**RP**	E	WHRD	CD	Prince William
47799	**RP**	E	WHRD	CD	Prince Henry

Class 47/4 ("47/8") Continued.

47802 +	**IS**	E	WNYX	CD(S)	
47805 +	**IS**	P	ILRA	TO	
47806 +	**V**	P	ILRA	TO	
47807 +	**V**	P	ILRA	TO	The Lion of Vienna
47810 +	**IS**	P	ILRA	TO	PORTERBROOK
47811 +	**GL**	P	IWLA	LE	
47812 +	**IS**	P	ILRA	TO	
47813 +	**GL**	P	IWLA	LE	S.S. Great Britain
47814 +	**V**	P	ILRA	TO	Totnes Castle
47815 +	**GL**	P	IWLA	LE	Abertawe Landore
47816 +	**GL**	P	IWLA	LE	Bristol Bath Road
					Quality Approved
47817 +	**V**	P	ILRA	TO	The Institution of Mechanical Engineers
47818 +	**V**	P	ILRA	TO	Strathclyde
47822 +	**V**	P	ILRA	TO	Pride of Shrewsbury
47826 +	**IS**	P	ILRA	TO	
47827 +	**V**	P	ILRA	TO	
47828 +	**IS**	P	ILRA	TO	
47829 +	**V**	P	ILRA	TO	
47830 +	**GL**	P	IWLA	LE	
47831 +	**V**	P	ILRA	TO	Bolton Wanderer
47832 +	**GL**	P	IWLA	LE	
47839 +	**V**	P	ILRA	TO	
47840 +	**V**	P	ILRA	TO	NORTH STAR
47841 +	**V**	P	ILRA	TO	Spirit of Chester
47843 +	**V**	P	ILRA	TO	VULCAN

47844 +	V	P	ILRA	TO	
47845 +	V	P	ILRA	TO	County of Kent
47846 +	GL	P	IWLA	LE	THOR
47847 +	IS	P	ILRA	TO	
47848 +	V	P	ILRA	TO	Newton Abbot Festival of Transport
47849 +	V	P	ILRA	TO	Cadeirlan Bangor Cathedral
47851 +	V	P	ILRA	TO	
47853 +	V	P	ILRA	TO	
47854 +	IS	P	ILRA	TO	Women's Royal Voluntary Service

CLASS 50   ENGLISH ELECTRIC   Co–Co

Built: 1967–68 by English Electric at Vulcan Foundry, Newton-le-Willows.
Engine: English Electric 16CVST of 2010 kW (2700 h.p.) at 850 r.p.m.
Main Generator: English Electric 840/4B.
Traction Motors: English Electric 538/5A.
Maximum Tractive Effort: 216 kN (48500 lbf).
Continuous Tractive Effort: 147 kN (33000 lbf) at 23.5 m.p.h.
Power At Rail: 1540 kW (2070 h.p.).   **Train Brakes:** Air & vacuum.
Brake Force: 59 t.   **Dimensions:** 20.88 x 2.78 x 3.96 m.
Weight: 116.9 t.   **Wheel Diameter:** 1092 mm.
Design Speed: 105 m.p.h.   **Maximum Speed:** 90 (* 100) m.p.h.
Fuel Capacity: 4796 litres.   **RA:** 6.
Train Supply: Electric, index 66.   **Multiple Working:** Orange Square.
Non-standard livery/numbering:
• 50017 is 'LMS Coronation Scot' style maroon with four gold bands.
• 50031 carries number D431.
• 50044 carries number D444.
• 50049 carries number D449.

50017 *	0	JK	MBDL	CQ	
50031	B	50	MBDL	KR	
50044	B	50	MBDL	KR	
50049	B	PD	MBDL	KR	
50050	BL	HS	SDFR	BH(S)	Fearless

CLASS 55   ENGLISH ELECTRIC   Co–Co

Built: 1961 by English Electric at Vulcan Foundry, Newton-le-Willows.
Engine: Two Napier-Deltic D18-25 of 1230 kW (1650 h.p.) each at 1500 r.p.m.
Main Generators: Two English Electric 829.
Traction Motors: English Electric 538/A.
Maximum Tractive Effort: 222 kN (50000 lbf).
Continuous Tractive Effort: 136 kN (30500 lbf) at 32.5 m.p.h.
Power At Rail: 1969 kW (2640 h.p.).   **Train Brakes:** Air & vacuum.
Brake Force: 51 t.   **Dimensions:** 21.18 x 2.68 x 3.94 m.
Weight: 104.7 t.   **Wheel Diameter:** 1092 mm.
Design Speed: 105 m.p.h.   **Maximum Speed:** 100 m.p.h.
Fuel Capacity: 3755 litres.   **RA:** 5.

Train Supply: Electric, index 66.   **Multiple Working:** Not equipped.
Non-standard livery/numbering:
- 55009 carries number D9009. Official RSL number is 89509.
- Official RSL number of 55019 is 89519.
- 55022 carries number D9000. Official RSL number is 89500.

55009	**GG**	DP	MBDL	CP	ALYCIDON
55019	**B**	DP	MBDL	CP	ROYAL HIGHLAND FUSILIER
55022	**GG**	90	SDFR	TM	ROYAL SCOTS GREY

CLASS 56   BRUSH/BR/PAXMAN   Co–Co

Built: 1976–84 by Electroputere at Craiova, Romania (as sub contractors for Brush) or BREL at Doncaster or Crewe Works.
Engine: Ruston Paxman 16RK3CT of 2460 kW (3250 h.p.) at 900 r.p.m.
Main Alternator: Brush BA1101A.
Traction Motors: Brush TM73-62.
Maximum Tractive Effort: 275 kN (61800 lbf).
Continuous Tractive Effort: 240 kN (53950 lbf) at 16.8 m.p.h.
Power At Rail: 1790 kW (2400 h.p.).   **Train Brakes:** Air.
Brake Force: 60 t.   **Dimensions:** 19.36 x 2.79 x 3.9 m.
Weight: 125.2 t.   **Wheel Diameter:** 1143 mm.
Design Speed: 80 m.p.h.   **Maximum Speed:** 80 m.p.h.
Fuel Capacity: 5228 litres.   **RA:** 7.
Train Supply: Not equipped.   **Multiple Working:** Red Diamond.
Note: All equipped with Slow Speed Control.

Non-standard livery:
- 56063 is as **F**, but with the light grey replaced by a darker grey.

56003	**LH**	E	WNXX	DD(S)	
56004	**B**	E	WNXX	OC(S)	
56006	**B**	E	WNXX	KR(S)	
56007	**T**	E	WGAI	IM	
56010	**T**	E	WNYX	DD(S)	
56011	**E**	E	WGAI	IM	
56018	**E**	E	WGAI	IM	
56019	**FQ**	E	WNYX	IM(S)	
56021	**LH**	E	WNXX	IM(S)	
56022	**T**	E	WNXX	IM(S)	
56025	**T**	E	WGAT	TE	
56027	**LH**	E	WGAT	TE	
56029	**T**	E	WNYX	DD(S)	
56031	**CE**	E	WGAI	IM	
56032	**E**	E	WGAI	IM	
56033	**T**	E	WGAI	IM	Shotton Paper Mill
56034	**LH**	E	WNYX	TT(S)	Castell Ogwr/Ogmore Castle
56036	**TC**	E	WNXX	CT(S)	
56037	**E**	E	WGAT	TE	
56038	**E**	E	WGAT	TE	
56039	**LH**	E	WNYX	TE(S)	
56040	**T**	E	WNXX	IM(S)	

56041	E	E	WGAI	IM	
56043	FM	E	WNXX	CT(S)	
56044	T	E	WGAI	IM	Cardiff Canton Quality Approved
56045	LH	E	WNXX	IM(S)	British Steel Shelton
56046	CE	E	WGAT	TE	
56047	TC	E	WNYX	IM(S)	
56048	CE	E	WGAT	TE	
56049	TC	E	WNXX	BW(S)	
56050	LH	E	WNYX	TT(S)	British Steel Teesside
56051	E	E	WGAT	TE	
56052	T	E	WNXX	DD(S)	
56053	T	E	WNXX	DD(S)	
56054	T	E	WGAT	TE	British Steel Llanwern
56055	LH	E	WGAT	TE	
56056	T	E	WGAT	TE	
56057	E	E	WNYX	IM(S)	British Fuels
56058	E	E	WGAT	TE	
56059	E	E	WGAI	IM	
56060	E	E	WGAT	TE	
56061	FM	E	WNYX	TT(S)	
56062	E	E	WGAI	IM	
56063	0	E	WGAT	TE	
56064	T	E	WNXX	CT(S)	
56065	E	E	WGAT	TE	
56066	T	E	WNYX	CF(S)	
56067	E	E	WGAT	TE	
56068	E	E	WGAT	TE	
56069	E	E	WGAI	IM	Wolverhampton Steel Terminal
56070	T	E	WNXX	BW(S)	
56071	E	E	WGAT	TE	
56072	T	E	WNXX	TO(S)	
56073	T	E	WGAT	TE	Tremorfa Steelworks
56074	LH	E	WGAI	IM	Kellingley Colliery
56075	F	E	WNYX	TT(S)	
56076	T	E	WNXX	IM(S)	
56077	LH	E	WNXX	CT(S)	
56078	F	E	WGAI	IM	
56079	T	E	WNXX	IM(S)	
56080	F	E	WNYX	SP(S)	Selby Coalfield
56081	E	E	WGAI	IM	
56082	F	E	WNXX	IM(S)	
56083	LH	E	WNXX	BW(S)	
56084	LH	E	WNXX	IM(S)	
56085	LH	E	WGAT	TE	
56086	T	E	WNXX	IM(S)	The Magistrates' Association
56087	E	E	WGAI	IM	ABP Port of Hull
56088	E	E	WGAI	IM	
56089	E	E	WGAT	TE	
56090	LH	E	WGAI	IM	
56091	E	E	WGAI	IM	Stanton
56093	T	E	WNXX	DD(S)	

56094	E	E	WGAT	TE	Eggborough Power Station
56095	E	E	WGAT	TE	
56096	E	E	WGAI	IM	
56098	F	E	WGAT	TE	
56099	T	E	WNXX	DD(S)	
56100	LH	E	WGAT	TE	
56101	T	E	WNXX	IM(S)	Mutual Improvement
56102	LH	E	WGAI	IM	
56103	E	E	WGAI	IM	STORA
56104	FC	E	WNXX	IM(S)	
56105	E	E	WGAT	TE	
56106	LH	E	WNXX	BW(S)	
56107	LH	E	WNXX	CT(S)	
56108	F	E	WNXX	TE(S)	
56109	LH	E	WNXX	CT(S)	
56110	LH	E	WGAI	IM	Croft[1]
56111	LH	E	WGAI	IM	
56112	LH	E	WGAI	IM	Stainless Pioneer
56113	E	E	WGAI	IM	
56114	E	E	WGAT	TE	
56115	E	E	WGAI	IM	
56116	LH	E	WGAI	IM	
56117	E	E	WGAT	TE	
56118	LH	E	WGAI	IM	
56119	E	E	WGAT	TE	
56120	E	E	WGAI	IM	
56121	T	E	WNYX	CU(S)	
56123	T	E	WNYX	IM(S)	Drax Power Station
56124	T	E	WNYX	KY(S)	
56125	F	E	WNXX	IM(S)	
56127	T	E	WGAT	TE	
56128	T	E	WNXX	IM(S)	
56129	T	E	WNXX	IM(S)	
56130	LH	E	WNXX	TT(S)	Wardley Opencast
56131	F	E	WGAI	IM	Ellington Colliery
56132	T	E	WNYX	TT(S)	
56133	F	E	WNXX	TT(S)	
56134	FC	E	WGAT	TE	Blyth Power
56135	F	E	WNYX	IM(S)	Port of Tyne Authority

CLASS 57   BRUSH/GM   Co–Co

Built: 1964–65 by Brush Traction at Loughborough or BR at Crewe Works as Class 47. Rebuilt 1997–2000 by Brush Traction at Loughborough.
Engine: General Motors 645-12E3 of 1860 kW (2500 h.p.) at 900 r.p.m.
Main Alternator: Brush BA1101A.
Traction Motors: Brush TM68-46.
Maximum Tractive Effort: 244.5 kN (55000 lbf).
Continuous Tractive Effort: 140 kN (31500 lbf) at ?? m.p.h.

Power at Rail: 1507 kW (2025 h.p.).   **Train Brakes:** Air.
Brake Force: 80 t.   **Dimensions:** 19.38 x 2.79 x 3.9 m.
Weight: 120.6 t.   **Wheel Diameter:** 1143 mm.
Design Speed: 75 m.p.h.   **Maximum Speed:** 75 m.p.h.
Fuel Capacity: 3273 (+ 5550 litres).   **RA:** 6
Train Supply: Not equipped.   **Multiple Working:** Not equipped.

57001	**FL**	P	DFHZ	FD	Freightliner Pioneer
57002	**FL**	P	DFHZ	FD	Freightliner Phoenix
57003	**FL**	P	DFHZ	FD	Freightliner Evolution
57004	**FL**	P	DFHZ	FD	Freightliner Quality
57005	**FL**	P	DFHZ	FD	Freightliner Excellence
57006	**FL**	P	DFHZ	FD	Freightliner Reliance
57007	**FL**	P	DFHZ	FD	Freightliner Bond
57008	**FL**	P	DFHZ	FD	Freightliner Explorer
57009	**FL**	P	DFHZ	FD	Freightliner Venturer
57010	**FL**	P	DFHZ	FD	Freightliner Crusader
57011	**FL**	P	DFHZ	FD	Freightliner Challenger
57012 +	**FL**	P	DFTZ	FD	Freightliner Envoy

Class 57/6. Electric Train Supply Equipment. Details as Class 57/0 except:

Fuel Capacity: 5887 litres.   **Train Supply:** Electric, index 95.

57601	(47825)	**P**	P	SBXL	LB(S)	Thomas Telford

CLASS 58   BREL/PAXMAN   Co–Co

Built: 1983–87 by BREL at Doncaster Works.
Engine: Ruston Paxman 12RK3ACT of 2460 kW (3300 h.p.) at 1000 r.p.m.
Main Alternator: Brush BA1101B.   **Traction Motors:** Brush TM73-62.
Maximum Tractive Effort: 275 kN (61800 lbf).
Continuous Tractive Effort: 240 kN (53950 lbf) at 17.4 m.p.h.
Power At Rail: 1780 kW (2387 h.p.).   **Train Brakes:** Air.
Brake Force: 62 t.   **Dimensions:** 19.13 x 2.72 x 3.93 m.
Weight: 130 t.   **Wheel Diameter:** 1120 mm.
Design Speed: 80 m.p.h.   **Maximum Speed:** 80 m.p.h.
Fuel Capacity: 4214 litres.   **RA:** 7.
Train Supply: Not equipped.   **Multiple Working:** Red Diamond.
Note: All equipped with Slow Speed Control.

58001	**MG** E	WNXX	KY(S)		
58002	**ML** E	WNXX	DI(S)	Daw Mill Colliery	
58003	**MG** E	WNXX	TT(S)	Markham Colliery	
58004	**MG** E	WNXX	DD(S)		
58005	**ML** E	WNXX	TO(S)	Ironbridge Power Station	
58006	**MG** E	WNXX	IW(S)		
58007	**MG** E	WNXX	IW(S)		
58008	**ML** E	WNXX	TT(S)		
58009	**MG** E	WFAN	TO		

58010	MG	E	WNXX	SF(S)	
58011	MG	E	WNXX	SF(S)	
58012	MG	E	WNXX	DD(S)	
58013	ML	E	WFAN	TO	
58014	ML	E	WNXX	TO(S)	Did.c.ot Power Station
58015	MG	E	WNXX	DD(S)	
58016	E	E	WFAN	TO	
58017	MG	E	WNXX	DD(S)	
58018	MG	E	WNXX	SF(S)	High Marnham Power Station
58019	MG	E	WFAN	TO	Shirebrook Colliery
58020	MG	E	WFAN	TO	Doncaster Works
58021	ML	E	WFAN	TO	Hither Green Depot
58022	MG	E	WNXX	DD(S)	
58023	ML	E	WNXX	DD(S)	
58024	E	E	WFAN	TO	
58025	MG	E	WFAN	TO	
58026	MG	E	WFAN	TO	
58027	MG	E	WNXX	DD(S)	
58028	MG	E	WNXX	TT(S)	
58029	MG	E	WFAN	TO	
58030	E	E	WFAN	TO	
58031	MG	E	WFAN	TO	
58032	ML	E	WNXX	SF(S)	Thoresby Colliery
58033	E	E	WFAN	TO	
58034	MG	E	WNXX	DD(S)	
58035	MG	E	WNXX	DD(S)	
58036	ML	E	WNXX	CD(S)	
58037	E	E	WFAN	TO	Worksop Depot
58038	ML	E	WNXX	TT(S)	
58039	E	E	WNXX	TT(S)	
58040	MG	E	WNXX	SF(S)	Cottam Power Station
58041	MG	E	WFAN	TO	Ratcliffe Power Station
58042	ML	E	WFAN	TO	
58043	MG	E	WFAN	TO	
58044	MG	E	WNXX	DD(S)	
58045	MG	E	WFAN	TO	
58046	ML	E	WNXX	LR(S)	Asfordby Mine
58047	E	E	WFAN	TO	
58048	E	E	WNXX	TT(S)	
58049	E	E	WFAN	TO	Littleton Colliery
58050	E	E	WFAN	TO	Toton Traction Depot

CLASS 59   GENERAL MOTORS   Co–Co

Built: 1985 (59001/002/004) or 1989 (59005) by General Motors, La Grange, Illinois, USA or 1990 (59101–4), 1994 (59201) and 1995 (59202–6) by General Motors, London, Ontario, Canada.
Engine: General Motors 645E3C two stroke of 2460 kW (3300 h.p.) at 900 r.p.m.

Main Alternator: General Motors AR11 MLD-D14A.
Traction Motors: General Motors D77B.
Maximum Tractive Effort: 506 kN (113 550 lbf).
Continuous Tractive Effort: 291 kN (65 300 lbf) at 14.3 m.p.h.
Power At Rail: 1889 kW (2533 h.p.).   **Train Brakes:** Air.
Brake Force: 69 t.   **Dimensions:** 21.35 x 2.65 x 3.9 m.
Weight: 121 t.   **Wheel Diameter:** 1067 mm.
Design Speed: 60 (* 75) m.p.h.   **Maximum Speed:** 60 (* 75) m.p.h.
Fuel Capacity: 4546 litres.   **RA:** 7.
Train Supply: Not equipped.   **Multiple Working:** AAR System.

Class 59/0. Owned by Foster-Yeoman.

59001	**FY**	FY	XYPO	MD	YEOMAN ENDEAVOUR
59002	**MR**	FY	XYPO	MD	ALAN J DAY
59004	**YO**	FY	XYPO	MD	PAUL A HAMMOND
59005	**FY**	FY	XYPO	MD	KENNETH J PAINTER

Class 59/1. Owned by Hanson Quarry Products.

59101	**HA**	HA	XYPA	MD	Village of Whatley
59102	**HA**	HA	XYPA	MD	Village of Chantry
59103	**HA**	HA	XYPA	MD	Village of Mells
59104	**HA**	HA	XYPA	MD	Village of Great Elm

Class 59/2. Owned by English Welsh & Scottish Railway.

59201 *	**E**	E	WDAG	HG	Vale of York
59202 *	**E**	E	WDAG	HG	Vale of White Horse
59203 *	**E**	E	WDAG	HG	Vale of Pickering
59204 *	**E**	E	WDAG	HG	Vale of Glamorgan
59205 b*	**E**	E	WDAG	HG	L. Keith McNair
59206 b*	**E**	E	WDAG	HG	Pride of Ferrybridge

CLASS 60   BRUSH/MIRRLEES   Co–Co

Built: 1989–1993 by Brush Traction at Loughborough.
Engine: Mirrlees 8MB275T of 2310 kW (3100 h.p.) at 1000 r.p.m.
Main Alternator: Brush BA1000.   **Traction Motors:** Brush TM216.
Maximum Tractive Effort: 500 kN (106500 lbf).
Continuous Tractive Effort: 336 kN (71570 lbf) at 17.4 m.p.h.
Power At Rail: 1800 kW (2415 h.p.).   **Train Brakes:** Air.
Brake Force: 74 (+ 62) t.   **Dimensions:** 21.34 x 2.64 x 3.95 m.
Weight: 129 (+ 131) t.   **Wheel Diameter:** 1118 mm.
Design Speed: 62 m.p.h.   **Maximum Speed:** 60 m.p.h.
Fuel Capacity: 4546 (+ 5225) litres. **RA:** 7.
Train Supply: Not equipped.   **Multiple Working:** Within class.
Note: All equipped with Slow Speed Control.
Non-standard livery:

- 60006 is in 'British Steel' livery of blue with white logos.
- 60033 is in 'Corus' livery of silver with red logos.
- 60064/070 are as **F**, with Loadhaul logos.

60001	E	E	WCAT	TE	
60002 +	E	E	WCAT	TE	High Peak
60003 +	E	E	WCAK	CF	FREIGHT TRANSPORT ASSOCIATION
60004 +	E	E	WCAK	CF	
60005 +	E	E	WCAK	CF	BP Gas Avonmouth
60006	O	E	WCAT	TE	Scunthorpe Ironmaster
60007 +	LH	E	WCAI	IM	
60008	LH	E	WCAT	TE	GYPSUM QUEEN II
60009 +	MG	E	WCAI	IM	Carnedd Dafydd
60010 +	E	E	WCAK	CF	
60011	ML	E	WCAT	TE	
60012 +	E	E	WCAI	IM	
60013	F	E	WCAT	TE	Robert Boyle
60014	FP	E	WCAT	TE	Alexander Fleming
60015 +	T	E	WCAK	CF	Bow Fell
60016	E	E	WCAN	TO	RAIL Magazine
60017 +	E	E	WCAT	TE	Shotton Works Centenary Year 1996
60018	E	E	WCAT	TE	
60019	E	E	WCAN	TO	
60020 +	E	E	WCAI	IM	
60021 +	F	E	WCAI	IM	Pen-y-Ghent[1]
60022 +	E	E	WCAI	IM	
60023 +	E	E	WCAI	IM	
60024 +	E	E	WCAN	TO	
60025 +	E	E	WCAI	IM	Caledonian Paper
60026 +	E	E	WCAK	CF	
60027 +	E	E	WCAI	IM	
60028 +	F	E	WCAI	IM	John Flamsteed
60029 +	E	E	WCAN	TO	Clitheroe Castle
60030 +	E	E	WCAK	CF	
60031	FM	E	WCAN	TO	
60032	T	E	WCAN	TO	William Booth
60033 +	O	E	WCAT	TE	Tees Steel Express
60034	T	E	WCAN	TO	Carnedd Llewelyn[1]
60035	T	E	WCAT	TE	Florence Nightingale
60036	E	E	WCAN	TO	GEFCO
60037 +	E	E	WCAK	CF	Aberthaw/Aberddawan
60038 +	LH	E	WCAI	IM	
60039	E	E	WCAT	TE	
60040	E	E	WCAT	TE	
60041 +	E	E	WCAK	CF	
60042 +	E	E	WCAT	TE	The Hundred of Hoo
60043	E	E	WCAT	TE	
60044	ML	E	WCAT	TE	
60045	E	E	WCAT	TE	The Permanent Way Institution
60046 +	F	E	WCAN	TO	William Wilberforce[1]
60047 +	E	E	WCAN	TO	
60048	E	E	WCAT	TE	EASTERN
60049 +	E	E	WCAT	TE	
60050 +	E	E	WCAT	TE	
60051 +	E	E	WCAK	CF	

60052 +	E	E	WCAK	CF	Glofa Twr - The last deep mine in Wales - Tower Colliery
60053 +	E	E	WCAT	TE	NORDIC TERMINAL
60054 +	FP	E	WCAN	TO	Charles Babbage
60055 +	T	E	WCAI	IM	Thomas Barnardo
60056 +	T	E	WCAK	CF	William Beveridge
60057	FC	E	WCAN	TO	Adam Smith
60058	T	E	WCAI	IM	John Howard
60059 +	LH	E	WCAK	CF	Swinden Dalesman
60060	FC	E	WCAT	TE	James Watt
60061	T	E	WCAT	TE	Alexander Graham Bell
60062	T	E	WCAT	TE	Samuel Johnson
60063	T	E	WCAT	TE	James Murray
60064 +	0	E	WCAK	CF	Back Tor[1]
60065	T	E	WCAT	TE	Kinder Low[1]
60066	FC	E	WCAN	TO	John Logie Baird
60067 +	F	E	WCAN	TO	James Clerk-Maxwell
60068	F	E	WCAN	TO	Charles Darwin
60069	F	E	WCAN	TO	Hum.p.h.ry Davy
60070 +	0	E	WCAK	CF	John Loudon McAdam
60071 +	MG	E	WCAN	TO	Dorothy Garrod
60072	MG	E	WCAN	TO	Cairn Toul[1]
60073	MG	E	WCAT	TE	Cairn Gorm[1]
60074	MG	E	WCAT	TE	
60075	MG	E	WCAN	TO	
60076	MG	E	WCAN	TO	
60077 +	MG	E	WCAK	CF	Canisp[1]
60078	ML	E	WCAT	TE	
60079	MG	E	WCAT	TE	Foinaven
60080 +	T	E	WCAI	IM	Kinder Scout
60081 +	GW	E	WCAK	CF	ISAMBARD KINGDOM BRUNEL
60082	T	E	WCAT	TE	Mam Tor
60083	E	E	WCAT	TE	Mountsorrel
60084	T	E	WCAN	TO	Cross Fell
60085	T	E	WCAT	TE	
60086	MG	E	WCAT	TE	Schiehallion
60087	MG	E	WCAN	TO	Slioch
60088	MG	E	WCAT	TE	Buachaille Etive Mor[1]
60089 +	T	E	WCAK	CF	Arcuil
60090 +	FC	E	WCAI	IM	Quinag
60091 +	FC	E	WCAK	CF	An Teallach
60092	F	E	WCAT	TE	Reginald Munns
60093	T	E	WCAT	TE	Jack Stirk
60094	MG	E	WCAN	TO	Tryfan
60095	F	E	WCAN	TO	
60096 +	T	E	WCAK	CF	Ben Macdui
60097 +	T	E	WCAI	IM	
60098 +	E	E	WCAK	CF	Charles Francis Brush
60099	MG	E	WCAT	TE	Ben More Assynt
60100	MG	E	WCAN	TO	Boar of Badenoch

CLASS 66   GENERAL MOTORS   Co–Co

Built: 1998–2000 by General Motors, London, Ontario, Canada (Model JT42CWR).
Engine: General Motors 12N-710G3B-EC two stroke of 2385 kW (3200 h.p.) at 900 r.p.m.
Main Alternator: General Motors AR8/C86.
Traction Motors: General Motors D43TR. **Maximum Tractive Effort:** 409 kN (92000 lbf).
Continuous Tractive Effort: 260 kN (58390 lbf) at 15.9 m.p.h.
Power At Rail: 1850 kW (2480 h.p.).   **Train Brakes:** Air.
Brake Force: 68 t.   **Dimensions:** 21.35 x 2.64 x 3.90 m.
Weight: 126 t.   **Wheel Diameter:** 1120 mm.
Design Speed: 75 m.p.h.   **Maximum Speed:** 75 m.p.h.
Fuel Capacity: 6550 litres.   **RA:** 7.
Train Supply: Not equipped.   **Multiple Working:** AAR System.
Note: All equipped with Slow Speed Control.

Class 66/0. EWS operated locomotives.

66001		E	A	WBAT	TE	66032 k	E	A	WBAK	CF
66002		E	A	WBAN	TO	66033		E	A	WBAH	EH
66003		E	A	WBAT	TE	66034		E	A	WBAH	EH
66004		E	A	WBAN	TO	66035		E	A	WBAM	ML
66005		E	A	WBAI	IM	66036 k	E	A	WBAI	IM
66006		E	A	WBAI	TE	66037 k	E	A	WBAN	TO
66007		E	A	WBAI	IM	66038		E	A	WBAN	TO
66008		E	A	WBAK	CF	66039 k	E	A	WBAI	IM
66009		E	A	WBAH	EH	66040		E	A	WBAN	TO
66010		E	A	WBAI	IM	66041		E	A	WBAT	TE
66011 k	E	A	WBAI	IM	66042		E	A	WBAN	TO
66012		E	A	WBAI	IM	66043		E	A	WBAK	CF
66013		E	A	WBAH	EH	66044		E	A	WBAT	TE
66014 k	E	A	WBAI	IM	66045 k	E	A	WBAI	IM
66015		E	A	WBAH	EH	66046		E	A	WBAI	IM
66016 k	E	A	WBAH	EH	66047 k	E	A	WBAT	TE
66017		E	A	WBAN	TO	66048		E	A	WBAI	IM
66018		E	A	WBAI	IM	66049		E	A	WBAM	ML
66019 k	E	A	WBAK	CF	66050		E	A	WBAI	IM
66020 k	E	A	WBAT	TE	66051		E	A	WBAT	TE
66021		E	A	WBAK	CF	66052		E	A	WBAI	IM
66022		E	A	WBAN	TO	66053		E	A	WBAI	IM
66023		E	A	WBAI	IM	66054		E	A	WBAK	CF
66024		E	A	WBAN	TO	66055		E	A	WBAK	CF
66025		E	A	WBAN	TO	66056		E	A	WBAK	CF
66026 k	E	A	WBAI	IM	66057		E	A	WBAK	CF
66027 k	E	A	WBAI	IM	66058		E	A	WBAK	CF
66028		E	A	WBAM	ML	66059		E	A	WBAN	TO
66029 k	E	A	WBAK	CF	66060		E	A	WBAI	IM
66030		E	A	WBAT	TE	66061		E	A	WBAH	EH
66031		E	A	WBAK	CF	66062		E	A	WBAN	TO

66063		E	A	WBAI	IM	66114 kr	E	A	WBBM	ML
66064		E	A	WBAH	EH	66115	E	A	WBAK	CF
66065		E	A	WBAM	ML	66116	E	A	WBAM	ML
66066		E	A	WBAM	ML	66117	E	A	WBAN	TO
66067		E	A	WBAN	TO	66118	E	A	WBAT	TE
66068		E	A	WBAI	IM	66119	E	A	WBAN	TO
66069		E	A	WBAI	IM	66120	E	A	WBAI	IM
66070		E	A	WBAT	TE	66121	E	A	WBAI	IM
66071		E	A	WBAI	IM	66122	E	A	WBAH	EH
66072		E	A	WBAI	IM	66123	E	A	WBAI	IM
66073		E	A	WBAI	IM	66124	E	A	WBAI	IM
66074		E	A	WBAN	TO	66125 k	E	A	WBAT	TE
66075		E	A	WBAN	TO	66126	E	A	WBAN	TO
66076		E	A	WBAK	CF	66127	E	A	WBAK	CF
66077		E	A	WBAI	IM	66128	E	A	WBAI	IM
66078		E	A	WBAT	TE	66129	E	A	WBAN	TO
66079		E	A	WBAK	CF	66130	E	A	WBAI	IM
66080		E	A	WBAK	CF	66131	E	A	WBAI	IM
66081		E	A	WBAI	IM	66132	E	A	WBAH	EH
66082		E	A	WBAH	EH	66133	E	A	WBAM	ML
66083		E	A	WBAT	TE	66134	E	A	WBAI	IM
66084 k		E	A	WBAI	IM	66135	E	A	WBAK	CF
66085		E	A	WBAI	IM	66136	E	A	WBAM	ML
66086		E	A	WBAN	TO	66137	E	A	WBAI	IM
66087		E	A	WBAN	TO	66138	E	A	WBAT	TE
66088		E	A	WBAK	CF	66139	E	A	WBAI	IM
66089		E	A	WBAT	TE	66140	E	A	WBAT	TE
66090		E	A	WBAK	CF	66141	E	A	WBAI	IM
66091		E	A	WBAI	IM	66142	E	A	WBAN	TO
66092		E	A	WBAK	CF	66143	E	A	WBAK	CF
66093		E	A	WBAT	TE	66144	E	A	WBAK	CF
66094 k		E	A	WBAI	IM	66145	E	A	WBAK	CF
66095 kr		E	A	WBBM	ML	66146	E	A	WBAH	EH
66096 r		E	A	WBBM	ML	66147	E	A	WBAI	IM
66097 r		E	A	WBBM	ML	66148	E	A	WBAN	TO
66098 r		E	A	WBBM	ML	66149	E	A	WBAT	TE
66099 r		E	A	WBBM	ML	66150	E	A	WBAN	TO
66100 r		E	A	WBBM	ML	66151	E	A	WBAK	CF
66101 r		E	A	WBBM	ML	66152	E	A	WBAM	ML
66102 kr		E	A	WBBM	ML	66153	E	A	WBAI	IM
66103 r		E	A	WBBM	ML	66154	E	A	WBAI	IM
66104 r		E	A	WBBM	ML	66155	E	A	WBAI	IM
66105 r		E	A	WBBM	ML	66156	E	A	WBAT	TE
66106 r		E	A	WBBM	ML	66157	E	A	WBAK	CF
66107		E	A	WBBM	ML	66158 k	E	A	WBAI	IM
66108 r		E	A	WBBM	ML	66159	E	A	WBAN	TO
66109 kr		E	A	WBBM	ML	66160	E	A	WBAI	IM
66110 r		E	A	WBBM	ML	66161	E	A	WBAT	TE
66111 r		E	A	WBBM	ML	66162	E	A	WBAH	EH
66112 r		E	A	WBBM	ML	66163	E	A	WBAN	TO
66113 r		E	A	WBBM	ML	66164	E	A	WBAK	CF

66165	k	E	A	WBAK	CF		66208	k	E	A	WBAN	TO
66166		E	A	WBAI	IM		66209	k	E	A	WBAI	IM
66167		E	A	WBAI	IM		66210	k	E	A	WBAN	TO
66168		E	A	WBAK	CF		66211	k	E	A	WBAT	TE
66169		E	A	WBAH	EH		66212	k	E	A	WBAK	CF
66170		E	A	WBAT	TE		66213	k	E	A	WBAI	IM
66171		E	A	WBAN	TO		66214	k	E	A	WBAK	CF
66172		E	A	WBAI	IM		66215	k	E	A	WBAK	CF
66173		E	A	WBAH	EH		66216	k	E	A	WBAH	EH
66174		E	A	WBAN	TO		66217	k	E	A	WBAH	EH
66175		E	A	WBAN	TO		66218	k	E	A	WBAN	TO
66176		E	A	WBAK	CF		66219	k	E	A	WBAN	TO
66177		E	A	WBAI	IM		66220	k	E	A	WBAI	IM
66178		E	A	WBAN	TO		66221	k	E	A	WBAI	IM
66179		E	A	WBAK	CF		66222	k	E	A	WBAK	CF
66180		E	A	WBAM	ML		66223	k	E	A	WBAT	TE
66181		E	A	WBAK	CF		66224	k	E	A	WBAT	TE
66182		E	A	WBAN	TO		66225	k	E	A	WBAN	TO
66183		E	A	WBAI	IM		66226	k	E	A	WBAI	IM
66184		E	A	WBAT	TE		66227	k	E	A	WBAT	TE
66185		E	A	WBAI	IM		66228	k	E	A	WBAI	IM
66186		E	A	WBAM	ML		66229	k	E	A	WBAK	CF
66187		E	A	WBAK	CF		66230	k	E	A	WBAI	IM
66188		E	A	WBAN	TO		66231	k	E	A	WBAN	TO
66189		E	A	WBAH	EH		66232	k	E	A	WBAN	TO
66190		E	A	WBAT	TE		66233	k	E	A	WBAT	TE
66191		E	A	WBAK	CF		66234	k	E	A	WBAI	IM
66192		E	A	WBAT	TE		66235	k	E	A	WBAK	CF
66193		E	A	WBAM	ML		66236	k	E	A	WBAK	CF
66194		E	A	WBAN	TO		66237	k	E	A	WBAI	IM
66195	k	E	A	WBAN	TO		66238	k	E	A	WBAH	EH
66196		E	A	WBAN	TO		66239	k	E	A	WBAK	CF
66197		E	A	WBAI	IM		66240	k	E	A	WBAI	IM
66198		E	A	WBAT	TE		66241	k	E	A	WBAK	CF
66199		E	A	WBAK	CF		66242	k	E	A	WBAI	IM
66200		E	A	WBAM	ML		66243	k	E	A	WBAN	TO
66201	k	E	A	WBAI	IM		66244	k	E	A	WBAT	TE
66202	k	E	A	WBAK	CF		66245	k	E	A	WBAI	IM
66203	k	E	A	WBAT	TE		66246	k	E	A	WBAN	TO
66204	k	E	A	WBAI	IM		66247	k	E	A	WBAN	TO
66205	k	E	A	WBAI	IM		66248	k	E	A	WBAM	ML
66206	k	E	A	WBAK	CF		66249	k	E	A	WBAH	EH
66207	k	E	A	WBAI	IM		66250	k	E	A	WBAK	CF

Class 66/5. Freightliner operated locomotives. Details as Class 66/0.

66501	**FL**	P	DFGM	FD	
66502	**FL**	P	DFGM	FD	
66503	**FL**	P	DFHH	FD	
66504	**FL**	P	DFHH	FD	
66505	**FL**	P	DFGM	FD	
66506	**FL**	H	DFRT	FD	Crewe Regeneration

66507	**FL**	H	DFRT	FD
66508	**FL**	H	DFRT	FD
66509	**FL**	H	DFRT	FD
66510	**FL**	H	DFRT	FD
66511	**FL**	H	DFGM	FD
66512	**FL**	H	DFGM	FD
66513	**FL**	H	DFGM	FD
66514	**FL**	H	DFGM	FD
66515	**FL**	H	DFGM	FD
66516	**FL**	H	DFGM	FD
66517	**FL**	H	DFGM	FD
66518	**FL**	H	DFGM	FD
66519	**FL**	H	DFGM	FD
66520	**FL**	H	DFGM	FD
66521		H		
66522		H		
66523		H		
66524		H		
66525		H		

Class 66/6. Freightliner operated locomotives with modified gear ratios.
Details as Classes 66/0 except:

Design Speed: 65 m.p.h.   **Maximum Speed:** 65 m.p.h.

66601	**FL**	P	DFHH	FD	The Hope Valley
66602	**FL**	P	DFHH	FD	
66603	**FL**	P	DFHH	FD	
66604	**FL**	P	DFHH	FD	
66605	**FL**	P	DFHH	FD	
66606	**FL**	P	DFHH	FD	

Class 66/7. GB Railfreight operated locomotives. Details as Class 66/0.

66701		H		
66702		H		
66703		H		
66704		H		
66705		H		
66706		H		
66707		H		

CLASS 67   GENERAL MOTORS   Bo–Bo

Built: 1999–2000 by Alstom at Valencia, Spain, as sub-contractors for General Motors (General Motors model JT42 HW-HS).
Engine: General Motors 12N-710G3B-EC two stroke of 2385 kW (3200 h.p.) at 900 r.p.m.
Main Alternator: General Motors AR9/HE3/CA6B.
Traction Motors: General Motors D43FM.
Maximum Tractive Effort: 141 kN (31750 lbf).
Continuous Tractive Effort: 90 kN (20200 lbf) at ?? m.p.h.

Power At Rail: 1860 kW.	**Train Brakes:** Air.
Brake Force: 78 t.	**Dimensions:** 19.74 x 2.72 x 3.95 m.
Weight: 90 t.	**Wheel Diameter:** 965 mm.
Design Speed: 125 m.p.h.	**Maximum Speed:** 110 m.p.h.
Fuel Capacity: 4927 litres.	**RA:** 8.
Train Supply: Electric, index 66.	**Multiple Working:** AAR System.

Note: All equipped with Slow Speed Control and Swinghead Knuckle automatic couplers.

67001	E	A	WAAK	CF	Night Mail
67002	E	A	WAAK	CF	Special Delivery
67003	E	A	WAAK	CF	
67004	E	A	WAAK	CF	Post Haste
67005	E	A	WAAK	CF	
67006	E	A	WAAK	CF	
67007	E	A	WAAK	CF	
67008	E	A	WAAK	CF	
67009	E	A	WAAK	CF	
67010	E	A	WAAK	CF	
67011	E	A	WAAK	CF	
67012	E	A	WAAK	CF	
67013	E	A	WAAK	CF	
67014	E	A	WAAK	CF	
67015	E	A	WAAK	CF	
67016	E	A	WAAK	CF	
67017	E	A	WAAK	CF	
67018	E	A	WAAK	CF	
67019	E	A	WAAK	CF	
67020	E	A	WAAK	CF	
67021	E	A	WAAK	CF	
67022	E	A	WAAK	CF	
67023	E	A	WHPT	CF	
67024	E	A	WAAK	CF	
67025	E	A	WAAK	CF	
67026	E	A	WAAK	CF	
67027	E	A	WAAK	CF	
67028	E	A	WAAK	CF	
67029	E	A	WAAK	CF	
67030	E	A	WAAK	CF	

2. ELECTRIC & ELECTRO-DIESEL LOCOS

CLASS 71   BR/ENGLISH ELECTRIC   Bo–Bo

Built: 1959 by BR at Doncaster Works.
Electric Supply System: 750 V d.c. from third rail.
Traction Motors: English Electric 532.
Maximum Tractive Effort: 195 kN (43800 lbf).
Continuous Rating: 1716 kW (2300 h.p.) giving a traction effort of 55 kN
(12400 lbf) at 69.6 m.p.h.   **RA:** 6.
Maximum Rail Power: 2239 kW (3000 h.p.).
Train Brakes: Air, vacuum & electro-pneumatic.
Brake Force: 41 t.   **Dimensions:** 15.42 x 2.82 x 3.99 m.
Weight: 76.2 t.   **Wheel Diameter:** 1219 mm.
Design Speed: 90 m.p.h.   **Maximum Speed:** 90 m.p.h.
Train Supply: Electric (300 kW maximum).
Multiple Working: SR System.
Non-standard livery/numbering:
•   71001 carries number E5001. Official RSL number is 89403.

71001	**G**	NR	MBEL	SE

CLASS 73   BR/ENGLISH ELECTRIC   Bo–Bo

Built: 1962 by BR at Eastleigh Works.
Engine: English Electric 4SRKT of 447 kW (600 h.p.) at 850 r.p.m.
Main Generator: English Electric 824/3D.
Electric Supply System: 750 V d.c. from third rail.
Traction Motors: English Electric 542A.
Maximum Tractive Effort: Electric 187 kN (42000 lbf).
Diesel 152 kN (34100 lbf).
Continuous Rating: Electric 1060 kW (1420 h.p.) giving a tractive effort of
43 kN (9600 lbf) at 55.5 m.p.h.
Continuous Tractive Effort: Diesel 72 kN (16100 lbf) at 10 m.p.h.
Maximum Rail Power: Electric 1830 kW (2450 h.p.) at 37 m.p.h.
Train Brakes: Air, vacuum & electro-pneumatic († Air & electro-pneumatic).
Brake Force: 31 t.   **Dimensions:** 16.36 x 2.64 x 3.8 m.
Weight: 76.3 t.   **Wheel Diameter:** 1016 mm.
Design Speed: 80 m.p.h.   **Maximum Speed:** 60 m.p.h.
Fuel Capacity: 1545 litres.   **RA:** 6.
Train Supply: Electric, index 66 (on electric power only). May also deliver a
reduced electric train supply when on diesel power whilst stationary.
Multiple Working: SR System.
Non-standard livery/numbering:
• 73005 is in non-standard blue livery with white roof.

Class 73/0. First build. Details as above.

73002	**BL**	ME	HEXX	KK(S)
73005	**0**	ME	HEXX	BD(S)

Class 73/1. Later build. Details as Class 73/0 except:

Built: 1965–67 by English Electric Co. at Vulcan Foundry, Newton le Willows.
Main Generator: English Electric 824/5D.
Traction Motors: English Electric 546/1B.
Maximum Tractive Effort: Electric 179 kN (40000 lbf).
                                           Diesel 160 kN (36000 lbf).
Continuous Rating: Electric 1060 kW (1420 h.p.) giving a tractive effort of
35 kN (7800 lbf) at 68 m.p.h.
Continuous Tractive Effort: Diesel 60 kN (13600 lbf) at 11.5 m.p.h.
Maximum Rail Power: Electric 2350 kW (3150 h.p.) at 42 m.p.h.
Weight: 77 t.   **Dimensions:** 16.36 x 2.64 x 3.81 m.
Design Speed: 90 m.p.h.   **Maximum Speed:** 60 (90*†) m.p.h.
Fuel Capacity: 1409 litres.
Train Supply: Electric, index 66 (on electric power only).

Note: ‡ Modified cabs for use on route learning duties.

73101	*	PC	E	WPAG	HG	The Royal Alex'
73103		I	E	WNXX	EH(S)	
73104	*	I	E	WNXX	EH(S)	
73105	*	CE	E	WNXX	OM(S)	
73106		DG	E	WNXX	HG(S)	
73107	*	CE	E	WNXX	OM(S)	Redhill 1844-1994
73108	*	CE	E	WPAG	HG	
73109	*	ST	SW	HYSB	BM	Battle of Britain 50th Anniversary
73110		CE	E	WPAG	HG	
73114	*	ML	E	WNXX	OM(S)	
73117		I	E	WNXX	EH(S)	University of Surrey
73118	†c	EP	EU	GPSN	OC	
73119	*	CE	E	WNXX	OM(S)	Kentish Mercury
73128	*	E	E	WPAG	HG	
73129	*	N	E	WPAG	HG	City of Winchester
73130	†c	EP	EU	GPSN	OC	
73131	*	E	E	WPAG	HG	
73132		I	E	WNXX	OM(S)	
73133	‡	ML	E	WPAG	HG	The Bluebell Railway
73134		I	E	WNXX	EH(S)	Woking Homes 1885-1985
73136	*	ML	E	WPAG	HG	Kent Youth Music
73138		CE	E	WNXX	OM(S)	
73139		I	E	WNXX	EH(S)	
73140		I	E	WNXX	OM(S)	
73141		I	E	WNXX	OM(S)	

Class 73/2. Locomotives originally dedicated to Gatwick Express-services.
Details as Class 73/1 except:

Maximum Speed: 90 m.p.h.   **Train Brakes:** Air & electro-pneumatic.

73201	GX	P	IVGA	SL
73202	GX	P	IVGA	SL
73203	GX	P	IVGA	SL
73204	GX	P	SBXL	SU(S)
73205	GX	P	IVGA	SL

73206	**GX**	P	IVGA	SL
73207	**GX**	P	IVGA	SL
73208	**GX**	P	IVGA	SL
73209	**GX**	P	IVGA	SL
73210	**GX**	P	IVGA	SL
73211	**GX**	P	IVGA	SL
73212	**GX**	RK	QXXX	ZA(S)
73213	**GX**	P	IVGA	SL
73235	**GX**	P	IVGA	SL

Class 73/9. Merseyrail Electrics operated locomotives. Details as Class 73/0.

73901	**MS**	ME	HEXX	BD(S)
73906	**MS**	ME	HEXX	BD(S)

NOTES FOR CLASSES 86–91

The following common features apply to all locos of Classes 86–92 unless otherwise stated.

Supply System: 25 kV a.c. 50 Hz overhead.
Multiple Working: Time division multiplex system.

CLASS 86   BR/ENGLISH ELECTRIC   Bo–Bo

Built: 1965–66 by English Electric Co. at Vulcan Foundry, Newton le Willows or by BR at Doncaster Works.
Traction Motors: AEI 282BZ frame mounted.
Maximum Tractive Effort: 207 kN (46500 lbf).
Continuous Rating: 3010 kW (4040 h.p.) giving a tractive effort of 85 kN (19200 lbf) at 77.5 m.p.h.
Maximum Rail Power: 4550 kW (6100 h.p.) at 49.5 m.p.h.
Train Brakes: Air.

Brake Force: 40 t.	**Dimensions:** 17.83 x 2.65 x 3.98 m.
Weight: 83–86.8 t.	**Wheel Diameter:** 1156 mm.
Design Speed: 100 m.p.h.	**Maximum Speed:** 100 m.p.h.
Train Supply: Electric, index 74.	**RA:** 6.

Class 86/1. Revised bogies and motors. Details as above except:

Maximum Tractive Effort: 258 kN (58000 lbf).
Traction Motors: GEC 412AZ.
Continuous Rating: 3730 kW (5000 h.p.) giving a TE of 95 kN (21300 lbf) at 87 m.p.h.
Maximum Rail Power: 5860 kW (7860 h.p.) at 50.8 m.p.h.

Weight: 86.8 t.	**Wheel Diameter:** 1150 mm.
Design Speed: 110 m.p.h.	**Maximum Speed:** 110 m.p.h.

86101		**IS**	H	SAXL	CE(S)	Sir William A Stanier FRS
86102		**IS**	H	SAXL	CE(S)	Robert A Riddles
86103	x	**IS**	H	SAXL	ZH(S)	André Chapelon

Class 86/2. Standard Design. Details as in main class heading except:
Weight: 85–86.2 t.
Note: 86243 is on loan to West Coast Train Care for operation by Virgin West Coast in pool IWPA.

86204	**IS**	H	SAXL	ZH(S)	City of Carlisle
86205	**IS**	H	IWPA	WN	City of Lancaster
86206	**V**	H	ICCA	LG	City of Stoke on Trent
86207	**IS**	H	ICCA	LG	City of Lichfield
86208	**IS**	E	WNXX	CE(S)	City of Chester
86209	**V**	H	SAXL	ZH(S)	City of Coventry
86210 x	**RX**	E	WNXX	CE(S)	C.I.T. 75th Anniversary
86212	**V**	H	ICCA	LG	Preston Guild 1328-1992
86213	**V**	H	SAXL	CQ(S)	Lancashire Witch
86214	**IS**	H	ICCA	LG	Sans Pareil
86215	**AR**	H	IANA	NC	
86216	**IS**	H	SAXL	ZH(S)	Meteor
86217	**AR**	H	IANA	NC	City University
86218	**AR**	H	IANA	NC	NHS 50
86219	**IS**	H	SAXL	ZH(S)	Phoenix
86220	**AR**	H	IANA	NC	The Round Tabler
86221	**AR**	H	IANA	NC	B.B.C. Look East
86222	**V**	H	ICCA	LG	Clothes Show Live
86223	**AR**	H	IANA	NC	Norwich Union
86224	**IS**	H	ICCA	LG	
86225	**V**	H	ICCA	LG	Hardwicke
86226	**V**	H	ICCA	LG	CHARLES RENNIE MACKINTOSH
86227	**IS**	H	SAXL	ZH(S)	Sir Henry Johnson
86228	**IS**	H	SAXL	CQ(S)	Vulcan Heritage
86229	**V**	H	IWPA	WN	Lions Clubs International
86230	**AR**	H	IANA	NC	
86231	**IS**	H	ICCA	LG	Starlight Express
86232	**AR**	H	IANA	NC	
86233	**V**	H	IWPA	WN	Laurence Olivier
86234	**IS**	H	ICCA	LG	J B Priestley OM
86235	**AR**	H	IANA	NC	Crown Point
86236	**V**	H	ICCA	LG	Josiah Wedgwood
86237	**AR**	H	IANA	NC	University of East Anglia
86238	**AR**	H	IANA	NC	European Community
86240	**V**	H	ICCA	LG	Bishop Eric Treacy
86241	**RX**	E	WNXX	CE(S)	Glenfiddich
86242	**V**	H	ICCA	LG	James Kennedy GC
86243 x	**RX**	E	WEOE	CE	
86244	**V**	H	ICCA	LG	The Royal British Legion
86245	**V**	H	IWPA	WN	Caledonian
86246	**AR**	H	IANA	NC	
86247	**V**	H	IWPA	WN	Abraham Darby
86248	**V**	H	ICCA	LG	Sir Clwyd/County of Clwyd
86249	**IS**	H	SAXL	CE(S)	County of Merseyside
86250	**AR**	H	IANA	NC	
86251	**V**	H	ICCA	LG	The Birmingham Post
86252	**AR**	H	IANA	NC	Sheppard 100

86253		IS	H	ICCA	LG	The Manchester Guardian
86254	x	RX	E	WNXX	CE(S)	
86255		IS	H	SAXL	ZH(S)	Penrith Beacon
86256		V	H	ICCA	LG	Pebble Mill
86257		AR	H	IANA	NC	
86258		V	H	ICCA	LG	
86259		V	H	IWPA	WN	Greater MANCHESTER
						THE LIFE & SOUL OF BRITAIN
86260		IS	H	IWPA	WN	Driver Wallace Oakes G.C.
86261	x	E	E	WEOE	CE	THE RAIL CHARTER PARTNERSHIP

Class 86/4. EWS owned locomotives. Details as Class 86/2 except:

Maximum Tractive Effort: 258 kN (58000 lbf).
Traction Motors: AEI 412AZ.   **Weight:** 83–83.9 t.
Continuous Rating: 2680 kW (3600 h.p.) giving a tractive effort of 89 kN (20000 lbf) at 67 m.p.h.
Maximum Rail Power: 4400 kW (5900 h.p.) at 38 m.p.h.

Note: 86424 is on loan to West Coast Train Care for operation by Virgin West Coast in pool IWPA.

86401		E	E	WEOE	CE	Hertfordshire Rail Tours
86416	x	RX	E	WEOE	CE	
86417	x	RX	E	WEOE	CE	
86419	x	RX	E	WNXX	CE(S)	
86424		RX	E	WEOE	CE	
86425		RX	E	WEOE	CE	Saint Mungo
86426	x	E	E	WEOE	CE	Pride of the Nation
86430	x	RX	E	WEOE	CE	Saint Edmund

Class 86/5. Regeared locomotive operated by Freightliner. Details as Class 86/2 except:

Maximum Tractive Effort: 258 kN (58000 lbf).
Traction Motors: AEI 282AZ.   **Weight:** 83–83.9 t.
Continuous Rating: 2680 kW (3600 h.p.) giving a tractive effort of 117 kN (26300 lbf) at 67 m.p.h.
Maximum Rail Power: 4400 kW (5900 h.p.) at 38 m.p.h.
Maximum Speed: 75 m.p.h.   **Train Supply:** Electric, isolated.

86501	(86608)	FL	FL	DFGC	FE	

Class 86/6. Freightliner operated locomotives. Details as Class 86/4 except:

Maximum Speed: 75 m.p.h.   **Train Supply:** Electric, isolated.

86602		FL	FL	DFNC	FE	
86603		FE	FL	DHLT	CE(S)	
86604		FF	FL	DFNC	FE	
86605		FF	FL	DFNC	FE	
86606		FF	FL	DFNC	FE	
86607		FL	FL	DFNC	FE	
86609		FL	FL	DFNC	FE	
86610		F	FL	DFNC	FE	
86611		FF	FL	DFNC	FE	Airey Neave

86612	FF	P	DFNC	FE	Elizabeth Garrett Anderson
86613	FL	P	DFNC	FE	
86614	FF	P	DFNC	FE	Frank Hornby
86615	F	P	DFNC	FE	Rotary International
86618	FF	P	DFNC	FE	
86620	FL	P	DFNC	FE	Philip G Walton
86621	FF	P	DFNC	FE	London School of Economics
86622	FF	P	DFNC	FE	
86623	FF	P	DFNC	FE	
86627	FL	P	DFNC	FE	
86628	FF	P	DFNC	FE	Aldaniti
86631	FL	P	DFNC	FE	
86632	FL	P	DFNC	FE	
86633	FF	P	DFNC	FE	Wulfruna
86634	FL	P	DFNC	FE	
86635	FL	P	DFNC	FE	
86636	FL	P	DHLT	CE(S)	
86637	FF	P	DFNC	FE	
86638	FF	P	DFNC	FE	
86639	FF	P	DFNC	FE	

CLASS 87　　　　　　　　　BREL/GEC　　　　　　　　Bo–Bo

Built: 1973–75 by BREL at Crewe Works.
Traction Motors: GEC G412AZ frame mounted.
Maximum Tractive Effort: 258 kN (58000 lbf).
Continuous Rating: 3730 kW (5000 h.p.) giving a TE of 95 kN (21300 lbf) at 87 m.p.h.
Maximum Rail Power: 5860 kW (7860 h.p.) at 50.8 m.p.h.
Train Brakes: Air.
Brake Force: 40 t.
Weight: 83.3 t.
Design Speed: 110 m.p.h.
Train Supply: Electric, index 95.
Dimensions: 17.83 x 2.65 x 3.96 m.
Wheel Diameter: 1150 mm.
Maximum Speed: 110 m.p.h.
RA: 6.

Class 87/0. Standard Design.

87001	V	P	IWCA	WN	Royal Scot
87002	V	P	IWCA	WN	Royal Sovereign
87003	V	P	IWCA	WN	Patriot
87004	V	P	IWCA	WN	Britannia
87005	V	P	IWCA	WN	City of London
87006	V	P	IWCA	WN	George Reynolds
87007	V	P	IWCA	WN	City of Manchester
87008	V	P	IWCA	WN	City of Liverpool
87009	V	P	IWCA	WN	City of Birmingham
87010	V	P	IWCA	WN	King Arthur
87011	V	P	IWCA	WN	
87012	V	P	IWCA	WN	
87013	V	P	IWCA	WN	John O'Gaunt
87014	V	P	IWCA	WN	Knight of the Thistle
87015	V	P	IWCA	WN	Howard of Effingham

87016	V	P	IWCA	WN	Willesden Intercity Depot
87017	V	P	IWCA	WN	Iron Duke
87018	V	P	IWCA	WN	Lord Nelson
87019	V	P	IWCA	WN	Sir Winston Churchill
87020	V	P	IWCA	WN	North Briton
87021	V	P	IWCA	WN	Robert The Bruce
87022	V	P	IWCA	WN	Lew Adams The Black Prince
87023	V	P	IWCA	WN	Polmadie
87024	V	P	IWCA	WN	Lord of the Isles
87025	V	P	IWCA	WN	County of Cheshire
87026	V	P	IWCA	WN	Sir Richard Arkwright
87027	V	P	IWCA	WN	Wolf of Badenoch
87028	V	P	IWCA	WN	Lord President
87029	V	P	IWCA	WN	Earl Marischal
87030	IS	P	IWCA	WN	Black Douglas
87031	V	P	IWCA	WN	Hal o' the Wynd
87032	V	P	IWCA	WN	Kenilworth
87033	V	P	IWCA	WN	Thane of Fife
87034	V	P	IWCA	WN	William Shakespeare
87035	V	P	IWCA	WN	Robert Burns

Class 87/1. Thyristor Control. Details as Class 87/0 except:
Traction Motors: GEC G412BZ frame mounted.
Continuous Rating: 3620 kW (4850 hp) giving a TE of 96 kN (21600 lbf) at 84 m.p.h.
Maximum Speed: 75 m.p.h.   **Weight:** 79.1 t.

87101	B	EF	WNXX	CE(S)	STEPHENSON

CLASS 89   BRUSH   Co–Co

Built: 1986 by BREL at Crewe Works (as sub-contractors for Brush).
Traction Motors: Brush. Frame mounted.
Maximum Tractive Effort: 205 kN (46000 lbf).
Continuous Rating: 4350 kW (5850 h.p.) giving a TE of 105 kN (23600 lbf) at 92 m.p.h.

Maximum Rail Power:	**Train Brakes:** Air.
Brake Force: 50 t.	**Dimensions:** 19.80 x 2.74 x 3.98 m.
Weight: 104 t.	**Wheel Diameter:** 1150 mm.
Design Speed: 125 m.p.h.	**Maximum Speed:** 125 m.p.h.
Train Supply: Electric, index 95.	**RA:** 6.

89001	GN	SI	IECB	BN	

CLASS 90   GEC   Bo–Bo

Built: 1987–90 by BREL at Crewe Works (as sub contractors for GEC).
Traction Motors: GEC G412CY frame mounted.
Maximum Tractive Effort: 258 kN (58000 lbf).
Continuous Rating: 3730 kW (5000 h.p.) giving a TE of 95 kN (21300 lbf) at 87 m.p.h.
Maximum Rail Power: 5860 kW (7860 h.p.) at 68.3 m.p.h.

Train Brakes: Air.
Brake Force: 40 (* 50) t.
Weight: 84.5 t.
Design Speed: 110 m.p.h.
Train Supply: Electric, index 95.
Non-standard liveries/numbering:

Dimensions: 18.80 x 2.74 x 3.97 m.
Wheel Diameter: 1156 mm.
Maximum Speed: 110 († 100) m.p.h.
RA: 7.

- 90029 is in German Federal Railways style red and white.
- 90036 is as **FE**, but has a yellow roof.

Class 90/0. Standard Design. Details as above.

Note: One (unspecified) locomotive is hired from EWS (Pool WEPE) to Great North Eastern Railway (Pool IECA) on a regular basis. This locomotive is used between London King's Cross and Leeds/Bradford Forster Square only.

90001	b	**V**	P	IWCA	WN	BBC Midlands Today
90002	b	**V**	P	IWCA	WN	Mission: Impossible
90003	b	**IS**	P	IWCA	WN	THE HERALD
90004	b	**V**	P	IWCA	WN	City of Glasgow
90005	b	**IS**	P	IWCA	WN	Financial Times
90006	b	**IS**	P	IWCA	WN	High Sheriff
90007	b	**IS**	P	IWCA	WN	Lord Stamp
90008	b	**IS**	P	IWCA	WN	The Birmingham Royal Ballet
90009	b	**V**	P	IWCA	WN	The Economist
90010	b	**IS**	P	IWCA	WN	275 Railway Squadron (Volunteers)
90011	b	**V**	P	IWCA	WN	West Coast Rail 250
90012	b	**V**	P	IWCA	WN	British Transport Police
90013	b	**V**	P	IWCA	WN	The Law Society
90014	b	**V**	P	IWCA	WN	
90015	b	**V**	P	IWCA	WN	The International Brigades SPAIN 1936-1939
90016	†b	**RX**	E	WEFE	CE	
90017	†b	**RX**	E	WEFE	CE	Rail Express Systems QualitY Assured
90018	†b	**RX**	E	WEFE	CE	
90019	†b	**RX**	E	WEFE	CE	Penny Black
90020	†b	**E**	E	WEFE	CE	Sir Michael Heron
90021	*	**FE**	EF	WEPE	CE	
90022	*	**FE**	EF	WEPE	CE	Freightconnection
90023	*	**FE**	EF	WEPE	CE	
90024	*	**GN**	EF	WEPE	CE	
90025	*	**FD**	EF	WEPE	CE	
90026	†	**FE**	EF	WEFE	CE	Crewe International Electric Maintenance Depot
90027	*	**FD**	EF	WEPE	CE	Allerton T & RS Depot Quality Approved
90028	†	**SB**	EF	WEPE	CE	Vrachtverbinding
90029	†	**O**	EF	WEPE	CE	Frachtverbindungen
90030	†	**E**	EF	WEPE	CE	Crewe Locomotive Works
90031	†	**E**	EF	WEPE	CE	The Railway Children Partnership Working For Children Worldwide
90032	†	**FE**	EF	WEPE	CE	Cerestar
90033	*	**FE**	EF	WEPE	CE	
90034	†	**FE**	EF	WEFE	CE	

90035	†	**FE**	EF	WEFE	CE
90036	†	**O**	EF	WEFE	CE
90037	†	**FD**	EF	WEFE	CE
90038	*	**FE**	EF	WEPE	CE
90039	*	**FD**	EF	WEPE	CE
90040	†	**FD**	EF	WEFE	CE

Class 90/1. Freightliner leased locomotives. Details as Class 90/0 except:

Maximum Speed: 75 m.p.h.   **Train Supply:** Electric, isolated.

Note: 90142 is on loan to West Coast Train Care for operation by Virgin West Coast (Pool IWCA) and has been temporarily reconfigured as Class 90/0.

90141	**FF**	P	DFLC	FE	
90142	**FF**	P	DFLC	FE	
90143	**FF**	P	DFLC	FE	Freightliner Coatbridge
90144	**FF**	P	DFLC	FE	
90145	**FF**	P	DFLC	FE	
90146	**FF**	P	DFLC	FE	
90147	**FF**	P	DFLC	FE	
90148	**FF**	P	DFLC	FE	
90149	**FF**	P	DFLC	FE	
90150	**FF**	P	DFLC	FE	

CLASS 91   GEC   Bo–Bo

Built: 1988–91 by BREL at Crewe Works (as sub contractors for GEC).
Traction Motors: GEC G426AZ.   **Cont. Rating:** 4540 kW (6090 h.p.).
Maximum Rail Power: 4700 kW (6300 h.p.).   **Train Brakes:** Air.
Brake Force: 45 t.   **Dimensions:** 19.41 x 2.74 x 3.76 m.
Weight: 84 t.   **Wheel Diameter:** 1000 mm.
Design Speed: 140 m.p.h.   **Maximum Speed:** 125 m.p.h.
Train Supply: Electric, index 95.   **RA:** 7.

Note: This class is in the process of refurbishment at Adtranz, Doncaster. Refurbished locomotives will be reclassified 91/1 and will be renumbered by the addition of 100 to their existing number.

91001	**GN**	H	IECA	BN	
91002	**GN**	H	IECA	BN	Durham Cathedral
91003	**GN**	H	IECA	BN	
91004	**GN**	H	IECA	BN	Grantham
91005	**GN**	H	IECA	BN	
91006	**GN**	H	IECA	BN	
91007	**GN**	H	IECA	BN	
91008	**GN**	H	IECA	BN	
91009	**GN**	H	IECA	BN	The Samaritans
91010	**GN**	H	IECA	BN	
91011	**GN**	H	IECA	BN	Terence Cuneo
91012	**GN**	H	IECA	BN	County of Cambridgeshire
91013	**GN**	H	IECA	BN	County of North Yorkshire
91014	**GN**	H	IECA	BN	St. Mungo Cathedral
91015	**GN**	H	IECA	BN	Holyrood

▲ Freightliner liveried Class 57 No. 57012 'Freightliner Envoy' enters Ipswich with the 16.35 Felixstowe South FLT–Ipswich on 5th May 2000.   **John Day**

▼ Class 58 No. 58041 'Ratcliffe Power Station', carrying two-tone grey livery with Mainline Freight branding, stands in Eastleigh East Yard with an engineers train on 19th December 1999.   **Brian Denton**

▲ Carrying the new Mendip Rail livery, Class 59 No. 59002 'Alan J. Day' approaches Fairwood Junction as it leaves Westbury with the 11.46 Fareham–Whatley Quarry stone empties. The date is 31st May 2000. **John Chalcraft**

▼ Mainline Freight liveried Class 60 No. 60078 forks left at Brocklesby Junction with the 11.24 Santon–Immingham on 28th May 1999. **Anthony Underwood**

▲ English Welsh & Scottish Railway liveried Class 66 No. 66014 stands with a train of box wagons at Liverpool's Gladstone Dock on 1st June 1999.

Paul Shannon

▼ The 14.30 London Victoria–Gatwick Airport Gatwick Express service passes through Selhurst on 29th April 2000 with Class 73 No. 73204 providing the power. These locomotives are in the process of being withdrawn from these services in favour of Class 460 EMUs.

K. Conkey

Class 67s Nos. 67014 and 67016, both in English Welsh & Scottish Railway livery, pass Colton Junction on 23rd August 2000 with a Low Fell to London Royal Mail service.

Ian A. Lyall

▲ Anglia Railways liveried Class 86 No. 86217 'City University' at Barham, near Ipswich with the 14.30 Norwich–London Liverpool Street on 25th February 2000.
Michael J. Collins

▼ Rail express systems liveried Class 86 No. 86243 takes a Low Fell to Bristol Temple Meads Royal Mail service through Durham on 26th July 1999.
Ian A. Lyall

Class 87 No. 87008, in Virgin Trains livery, approaches Winwick Junction on 6th May 2000 with the 13.30 London Euston–Preston. **Paul Senior**

▲ Great North Eastern Railway liveried Class 89 No. 89001 waits to depart from Leeds with the 10.05 to London Kings Cross on 25th May 1999.   **G.W. Morrison**

▼ Class 90 No. 90145 hauls a southbound Freightliner at Greenholme during July 1998. The loco carries the old two-tone grey Freightliner colours now superceded by the green and yellow livery.   **Dave McAlone**

▲ The 07.00 London King Cross–Edinburgh races past Eaton Lane, Retford behind Great North Eastern Railway liveried Class 91 No. 91031 on 26th July 1999.
Ian A. Lyall

▼ European Passenger Services liveried Class 92 No. 92024 'J S Bach' coasts downgrade from Shap summit at Orton Moor on 27th August 1999 with the 14.48 Mossend Yard–Eastleigh Enterprise service.
Dave McAlone

91016	**GN**	H	IECA	BN	
91017	**GN**	H	IECA	BN	City of Leeds
91018	**GN**	H	IECA	BN	Bradford Film Festival
91019	**GN**	H	IECA	BN	County of Tyne & Wear
91020	**GN**	H	IECA	BN	
91021	**GN**	H	IECA	BN	Archbishop Thomas Cranmer
91022	**GN**	H	IECA	BN	Double Trigger
91023	**GN**	H	IECA	BN	
91024	**GN**	H	IECA	BN	
91025	**GN**	H	IECA	BN	Berwick-upon-Tweed
91026	**GN**	H	IECA	BN	York Minster
91127	**GN**	H	IECA	BN	
91028	**GN**	H	IECA	BN	Peterborough Cathedral
91029	**GN**	H	IECA	BN	Queen Elizabeth II
91030	**GN**	H	IECA	BN	
91031	**GN**	H	IECA	BN	County of Northumberland

CLASS 92   BRUSH   Co–Co

Built: 1993–96 by Brush Traction at Loughborough.
Supply System: 25 kV a.c. 50 HZ overhead or 750 V d.c. third rail.
Traction Motors: Brush.
Maximum Tractive Effort: 400 kN (90 000 lbf).
Continuous Rating: 5040 kW (6760 h.p.) on a.c., 4000 kW (5360 h.p.) on d.c.
Maximum Rail Power: **Train Brakes:** Air.
Brake Force: 63 t.   **Dimensions:** 21.34 x 2.67 x 3.96 m.
Weight: 126 t.   **Wheel Diameter:** 1160 mm.
Design Speed: 140 km/h (87½ m.p.h.).
Maximum Speed: 140 km/h (87½ m.p.h.).
Train Supply: Electric, index 108 (a.c.), 70 (d.c.).   **RA:** 7.

Note: Locomotives in pool WTWE are also authorised to operate on the Eurotunnel network.. These locomotives have temporarily had their d.c. shoegear removed and may only operate under power between Dollands Moor and Fréthun.

92001	**E**	E	WTWE	CE	Victor Hugo
92002	**EP**	E	WTWE	CE	H.G. Wells
92003	**EP**	E	WTWE	CE	Beethoven
92004	**EP**	E	WTAE	CE	Jane Austen
92005	**EP**	E	WTAE	CE	Mozart
92006	**EP**	SF	WTAE	CE	Louis Armand
92007	**EP**	E	WTAE	CE	Schubert
92008	**EP**	E	WTAE	CE	Jules Verne
92009	**EP**	E	WTAE	CE	Elgar
92010	**EP**	SF	WTWE	CE	Molière
92011	**EP**	E	WTAE	CE	Handel
92012	**EP**	E	WTWE	CE	Thomas Hardy
92013	**EP**	E	WTAE	CE	Puccini
92014	**EP**	SF	WTAE	CE	Emile Zola
92015	**EP**	E	WTAE	CE	D.H. Lawrence
92016	**EP**	E	WTAE	CE	Brahms
92017	**EP**	E	WTAE	CE	Shakespeare

92018	**EP**	SF	WTAE	CE	Stendhal
92019	**EP**	E	WTAE	CE	Wagner
92020	**EP**	EU	WTAE	CE	Milton
92021	**EP**	EU	WTAE	CE	Purcell
92022	**EP**	E	WTAE	CE	Charles Dickens
92023	**EP**	SF	WTAE	CE	Ravel
92024	**EP**	E	WTAE	CE	J.S. Bach
92025	**EP**	E	WTAE	CE	Oscar Wilde
92026	**EP**	E	WTAE	CE	Britten
92027	**EP**	E	WTWE	CE	George Eliot
92028	**EP**	SF	WTWE	CE	Saint Saëns
92029	**EP**	E	WTWE	CE	Dante
92030	**EP**	E	WTWE	CE	Ashford
92031	**EP**	E	WTWE	CE	
92032	**EP**	EU	WTAE	CE	César Franck
92033	**EP**	SF	WTAE	CE	Berlioz
92034	**EP**	E	WTAE	CE	Kipling
92035	**EP**	E	WTAE	CE	Mendelssohn
92036	**EP**	E	WTAE	CE	Bertolt Brecht
92037	**EP**	E	WTWE	CE	Sullivan
92038	**EP**	SF	WTWE	CE	Voltaire
92039	**EP**	E	WTWE	CE	Johann Strauss
92040	**EP**	EU	WTWE	CE	Goethe
92041	**EP**	E	WTAE	CE	Vaughan Williams
92042	**EP**	E	WTAE	CE	Honegger
92043	**EP**	SF	WTWE	CE	Debussy
92044	**EP**	EU	WTAE	CE	Couperin
92045	**EP**	EU	WTWE	CE	Chaucer
92046	**EP**	EU	WTAE	CE	Sweelinck

UNCLASSIFIED   METROPOLITAN VICKERS   Bo–Bo

Built: 1922 by Metropolitan Vickers at Gorton.
Electric Supply System: 750 V d.c. from third rail or four rail system.
Traction Motors:
Maximum Tractive Effort: 100 kN (22600 lbf).
Continuous Rating: 895 kW (1200 h.p.) giving a tractive effort of 65 kN (14700 lbf) at ? m.p.h.
Maximum Rail Power:
Brake Force:
Weight: 76.2 t.
Design Speed: 65 m.p.h.
Train Supply: Not equipped.
Non-standard livery/numbering:

RA:
Train Brakes: Air.
Dimensions:
Wheel Diameter: 1105 mm.
Maximum Speed: 65 m.p.h.
Multiple Working: Not equipped.

- 12 is London Transport livery of maroon, lined out in straw with red window surrounds and solebar. Official RSL number is 89212.

| 12 | **0** | LU | MBEL | WR | SARAH SIDDONS |

3. MISCELLANEOUS VEHICLES

CLASS 37 POWER UNIT TRANSPORTER/ MAINTENANCE VEHICLE

Built: 1962-63 by English Electric Company at Vulcan Foundry, Newton le Willows (025031) or by Robert Stephenson & Hawthorn at Darlington (025032). Converted to power unit transporter/maintenance vehicle in 1996 at Toton TMD. Also carry local numbers 1 & 2 respectively. Stored out of use since cessation of Class 37 overhauls by EWS.

025031	**DG**	E	TO(S)
025032	**DG**	E	TO(S)

4. LOCOMOTIVES AWAITING DISPOSAL

The list below comprises locomotives awaiting disposal which are stored on the Railtrack network, together with locomotives stored at other locations (e.g. private repair facilites) which, although awaiting disposal, remain Railtrack registered. This includes locomotives for which sales have been agreed, but collection by the new owner had not been made at the time of going to press.

Non-standard liveries/numbering:
- 20092, 20169 and 47972 are in British Railways Board Central Services livery of red and grey.
- 37101 is officially numbered 37345, but it is doubtful it has ever carried this number.
- 37137 is being used for painting trials, hence livery carried may vary from time to time.
- 43173 is in Great Western Trains livery of Green and ivory.
- 47803 is yellow and white with a red stripe.

08473	**B**	X	WNZX	LR		20073	**B**	HN	HNRL	BS
08515	**B**	X	WNZX	GD		20081	**B**	HN	HNRL	BS
08517	**B**	X	WNZX	SF		20092	**O**	HN	HNRL	BS
08594	**B**	PO	WNZX	ZB		20119	**B**	E	WNZX	TT
08618	**B**	X	WNZX	GD		20121	**B**	DR	XHSS	ZB
08622	**B**	PO	WNZX	ML		20138	**FQ**	HN	HNRL	BS
08634	**B**	X	WNZX	SF		20168	**B**	E	WNZX	MG
08700	**B**	X	WNZX	SF		20169	**O**	PO	WNZX	BS
08731	**B**	PO	WNZX	ML		20177	**B**	E	WNZX	TT
08826	**B**	PO	WNZX	ML		31102	**CE**	PO	WNZX	CD
08855	**B**	E	WNZX	ZB		31125	**CE**	HN	HNRL	BS
20007	**B**	DR	XHSS	ZB		31168	**B**	HN	HNRL	BS
20016	**B**	HN	HNRL	BS		31174	**CE**	HN	HNRL	BS
20032	**B**	DR	XHSS	ZB		31196	**CE**	X	WNZX	SF
20059	**FQ**	E	WNZX	MG		31200	**CE**	E	WNZX	CW
20066	**B**	HN	HNRL	BS		31229	**CE**	HN	HNRL	BS
20072	**B**	DR	XHSS	ZB		31263	**CE**	HN	HNRL	BS

31273	CE	X	WNZX	HM	37209	BL	E	WNZX	DD
31275	F	E	WNZX	CS	37213	FC	E	WNZX	TT
31282	FQ	HN	HNRL	BS	37214	T	E	WNZX	SP
31283	B	X	WNZX	SF	37218	F	E	WNZX	IM
31286	B	HN	HNRL	BS	37222	MG	E	WNZX	CF
31296	FA	E	WHZX	CP	37223	FC	E	WNZX	IM
31299	FO	X	WNZX	SF	37227	MG	X	WNZX	OM
31319	FC	PO	WNZX	CW	37229	FC	E	WNZX	CF
31320	B	X	WNZX	SF	37235	F	E	WNZX	DD
31407	ML	E	WNZX	BS	37240	CE	E	WNZX	SP
31408	B	E	WNZX	SP	37242	ML	E	WNZX	SP
31410	RR	E	WNZX	CS	37244	F	E	WNZX	SP
31411	DG	E	WNZX	BS	37251	IS	PO	WNZX	SP
31417	DG	E	WNZX	BS	37254	CE	X	WNZX	ZH
31421	RR	PO	WNZX	CW	37255	CE	E	WNZX	SP
31428	B	HN	HNRL	BS	37278	FC	E	WNZX	TT
31432	B	E	WNZX	SP	37340	FD	E	WNZX	IM
31442	B	E	WNZX	CQ	37343	CE	E	WNZX	TT
31444	CE	E	WNZX	SP	37359	FP	E	WNZX	TE
31516	CE	E	WNZX	BS	37380	MG	E	WNZX	CD
31519	CE	HN	HNRL	BS	37384	CE	E	WNZX	SP
31541	CE	E	WNZX	OM	37404	T	E	WNZX	SP
31545	B	E	WNZX	BS	37904	FM	E	WNZX	CF
31548	CE	HN	HNRL	BS	43173	0	A	SCXL	PY
33038	B	X	WHZX	SF	45015	B	E	WNZX	TT
33205	FD	X	WNZX	OC	47033	FE	EF	WNZX	SP
37012	CE	E	WNZX	SP	47125	FE	PO	WNZX	CW
37019	FD	E	WNZX	HM	47156	FD	EF	WNZX	CW
37043	TC	E	WNZX	SP	47194	FD	EF	WNZX	SP
37045	F	E	WNZX	TT	47223	F	E	WNZX	CW
37048	MG	E	WNZX	TT	47238	FD	X	WNZX	BS
37063	FD	HN	HNRL	ZB	47276	F	EF	WNZX	SP
37068	FD	E	WNZX	IM	47294	FD	E	WNZX	TT
37072	DG	HN	HNRL	ZB	47297	FE	EF	WNZX	SP
37078	FM	E	WNZX	SP	47300	CE	E	WNZX	SP
37079	FD	X	WNZX	ZH	47341	CE	E	WNZX	TT
37088	TC	E	WNZX	SP	47344	FE	EF	WNZX	SP
37095	CE	X	WNZX	ZH	47351	FE	EF	WNZX	SP
37098	CE	X	WNZX	OM	47355	FD	EF	WNZX	HM
37101	FD	E	WHZX	IM	47363	F	EF	WNZX	SP
37137	0	E	WNZX	TT	47484	GW	E	WNZX	CD
37139	FC	E	WNZX	TE	47565	RX	E	WNZX	SP
37140	CE	E	WNZX	SP	47628	RX	E	WNZX	CW
37141	CE	E	WNZX	CD	47704	RX	E	WNZX	CD
37142	CE	E	WNZX	CW	47803	0	E	WNZX	SF
37144	FA	E	WNZX	IM	47971	BL	E	WNZX	ZC
37153	TC	E	WNZX	SP	47972	0	E	WNZX	CD
37188	TC	E	WNZX	TT	56023	FC	E	WNZX	TT
37191	CE	E	WNZX	SP	56092	T	E	WNZX	SP
37201	TC	E	WNZX	BS	56097	FM	E	WNZX	SP

5. LOCOMOTIVES UNDERGOING RECERTIFICATION

The following locomotives are currently undergoing or have recently undergone restoration with a view to receiving Railtrack certification.

Non-standard liveries/numbering:
• 08168 is in black livery.

03170	**B**	HN	BH	20206	**B** MO	ZB
07001	**HN**	HN	BH	31105	**T** FR	BH
07013	**B**	HN	BH	31106	**CE** HJ	ZA
08168	**O**	PO	ZA	31107	**CE** HJ	BH
08359	**G**	PO	TS	31128	**FO** PO	TM
08507	**B**	HN	BH	31439	**RR** FR	ZA
08750	**B**	RT	ZB	31461	**DG** FR	TM
08936	**B**	HN	BH	31537	**CE** FR	ZA
12082	**HN**	HN	BH	33108	**B** PO	TM
20057	**B**	HN	BS	33207	**HN** HN	ZA
20132	**B**	HN	BS	45112	**B** PO	TM
20165	**FO**	DR	KD			

6. EUROTUNNEL LOCOMOTIVES

DIESEL LOCOMOTIVES

0001–0005   MaK   Bo-Bo

Built: 1992–93 by MaK at Kiel, Germany (Model DE1004).
Engine: MTU 12V 396 Tc of 1180 kW (1580 h.p.) at 1800 rpm.
Main Alternator: BBC.   **Traction Motors:** BBC.
Maximum Tractive Effort: 305 kN (68600 lbf).
Continuous Tractive Effort: 140 kN (31500 lbf) at 20 mph.
Power At Rail: 750 kW (1012 h.p.).

Brake Force: 120 kN.	**Dimensions:** 16.50 x ?? x ?? m.
Weight: 84 t.	**Wheel Diameter:** 1000 mm.
Design Speed: 120 km/h.	**Maximum Speed:** 120 km/h.
Fuel Capacity:	**Train Brakes:** Air.
Train Supply: Not equipped.	**Multiple Working:** Within class.

0001	**GY**	ET	CO
0002	**GY**	ET	CO
0003	**GY**	ET	CO
0004	**GY**	ET	CO
0005	**GY**	ET	CO

0032–0042   HUNSLET/SCHÖMA   0–4–0

Built: 1989–90 by Hunslet Engine Company at Leeds as 900 mm. gauge.
Rebuilt: 1993-94 by Schöma in Germany to 1435 mm. gauge.
Engine: Deutz of 270 kW (200 h.p.) at ???? rpm.

Transmission: Mechanical.	**Maximum Tractive Effort:**
Cont. Tractive Effort:	**Power At Rail:**
Brake Force:	**Dimensions:**
Weight:	**Wheel Diameter:**
Design Speed: 50 km/h.	**Maximum Speed:** 50 km/h.
Fuel Capacity:	**Train Brakes:** Air.
Train Supply: Not equipped.	**Multiple Working:** Not equipped.

0031	**Y**	ET	CO	FRANCES
0032	**Y**	ET	CO	ELISABETH
0033	**Y**	ET	CO	SILKE
0034	**Y**	ET	CO	AMANDA
0035	**Y**	ET	CO	MARY
0036	**Y**	ET	CO	LAWRENCE
0037	**Y**	ET	CO	LYDIE
0038	**Y**	ET	CO	JENNY
0039	**Y**	ET	CO	PACITA
0040	**Y**	ET	CO	JILL
0041	**Y**	ET	CO	KIM
0042	**Y**	ET	CO	NICOLE

ELECTRIC LOCOMOTIVES

9001–9108 BRUSH/ABB Bo-Bo-Bo

Built: 1993–2000 by Brush Traction at Loughborough.
Supply System: 25 kV a.c. 50 Hz overhead.
Traction Motors: ABB 6PH. **Maximum Tractive Effort:** 400 kN (90 000 lbf).
Continuous Rating: 5760 kW (7725 h.p.) giving a TE of 310 kN at 65 km/h.
Maximum Rail Power: **Multiple Working:** TDM system.
Brake Force: 50 t. **Dimensions:** 22.01 x 2.97 x 4.20 m.
Weight: 132 t. **Wheel Diameter:** 1090 mm.
Design Speed: 175 km/h. **Maximum Speed:** 160 km/h.
Train Supply: Electric. **Train Brakes:** Air.

CLASS 9/0. Mixed traffic locomotives.

9001	**ET**	ET	CO	LESLEY GARRETT
9002	**ET**	ET	CO	STUART BURROWS
9003	**ET**	ET	CO	BENJAMIN LUXON
9004	**ET**	ET	CO	VICTORIA DE LOS ANGELES
9005	**ET**	ET	CO	JESSYE NORMAN
9006	**ET**	ET	CO	REGINE CRESPIN
9007	**ET**	ET	CO	DAME JOAN SUTHERLAND
9008	**ET**	ET	CO	ELISABETH SODERSTROM
9009	**ET**	ET	CO	FRANÇOIS POLLET
9010	**ET**	ET	CO	JEAN-PHILLIPE COURTIS
9011	**ET**	ET	CO	JOSÉ VAN DAM
9012	**ET**	ET	CO	LUCIANO PAVAROTTI
9013	**ET**	ET	CO	MARIA CALLAS
9014	**ET**	ET	CO	LUCIA POPP
9015	**ET**	ET	CO	LÖTSCHBERG 1913
9016	**ET**	ET	CO	WILLARD WHITE
9017	**EG**	ET	CO	JOSÉ CARRERAS
9018	**ET**	ET	CO	WILHELMENA FERNANDEZ
9019	**ET**	ET	CO	MARIA EWING
9020	**ET**	ET	CO	Nicolai Ghiaurov
9021	**ET**	ET	CO	TERESA BERGANZA
9022	**ET**	ET	CO	DAME JANET BAKER
9023	**ET**	ET	CO	DAME ELISABETH LEGGE-SCHWARZKOPF
9024	**ET**	ET	CO	GOTTHARD 1882
9025	**ET**	ET	CO	JUNGFRAUJOCH 1912
9026	**ET**	ET	CO	FURKATUNNEL 1982
9027	**ET**	ET	CO	BARBARA HENDRICKS
9028	**ET**	ET	CO	DAME KIRI TE KANAWA
9029	**ET**	ET	CO	THOMAS ALLEN
9031	**ET**	ET	CO	
9032	**ET**	ET	CO	RENATA TEBALDI
9033	**ET**	ET	CO	MONTSERRAT CABALLE
9034	**ET**	ET	CO	MIRELLA FRENI
9035	**ET**	ET	CO	Nicolai Gedda

9036	**ET**	ET	CO	ALAIN FONDARY
9037	**ET**	ET	CO	GABRIEL BACQUIER
9038	**ET**	ET	CO	HILDEGARD BEHRENS
9040	**EG**	ET	CO	

CLASS 9/1. Freight Shuttle dedicated locomotives.

9101	**EG**	ET	CO
9102	**EG**	ET	CO
9103	**EG**	ET	CO
9104	**EG**	ET	CO
9105	**EG**	ET	CO
9106	**EG**	ET	CO
9107	**EG**	ET	CO
9108			

9201–9207   BRUSH/ADTRANZ   Bo-Bo-Bo

Built: 2000–01 by Brush Traction at Loughborough.
Supply System: 25 kV a.c. 50 Hz overhead.

Traction Motors:	**Maximum Tractive Effort:**
Continuous Rating:	
Maximum Rail Power:	**Multiple Working:**
Brake Force:	**Dimensions:**
Weight:	**Wheel Diameter:**
Design Speed:	**Maximum Speed:**
Train Supply:	**Train Brakes:**

9201
9202
9203
9204
9205
9206
9207

7. CODES

LIVERY CODES

* denotes an obsolescent livery style no longer normally used for repaints.

Code	Description
AR	Anglia Railways (Turquoise blue with white stripe).
B*	BR (Blue).
BL*	BR (Blue with yellow cabs, grey roof, large numbers).
BR*	BR (Blue with red solebar stripe).
CE*	BR Engineers (Yellow & grey with black cab doors and window surrounds).
CX	Connex (White with yellow lower body and blue solebar).
DG*	BR Departmental (Plain dark grey with black cab doors and window surrounds).
DR	Direct Rail Services (Dark blue with light blue roof).
E	English Welsh & Scottish Railway (Maroon bodyside & roof with gold stripe, gold reflective stripe at solebar level).
EG	Eurotunnel (Two-tone grey and white).
EN	Enron Teesside Operations (Trafalgar blue with red solebar stripe).
EP	European Passenger Services (Two-tone grey with dark blue roof).
ET	Eurotunnel (Two-tone grey and white with green and blue bands).
F*	BR Trainload Freight (Two-tone grey with black cab doors and window surrounds. No logos).
FA*	BR Trainload Construction (Two-tone grey with black cab doors and window surrounds. Yellow & blue chequered logo).
FC*	BR Trainload Coal (Two-tone grey with black cab doors and window surrounds. Black & yellow logo).
FD*	BR Railfreight Distribution (Two-tone grey with black cab doors and window surrounds. Yellow & red logo).
FE*	Railfreight Distribution International (Two tone-grey with black cab doors and dark blue roof. Red & yellow logo).
FF*	Freightliner (Two-tone grey with black cab doors and window surrounds. Freightliner logo).
FG	First Great Western (green and ivory with thin green and broad gold stripes).
FL	Freightliner (Dark green with yellow cabs).
FM*	BR Trainload Metals (Two-tone grey with black cab doors and window surrounds. Yellow & blue chevrons logo).
FO*	BR Railfreight (Grey bodyside, yellow cabs, red buffer beam, large double-arrow logo).
FP*	BR Trainload Petroleum (Two-tone grey with black cab doors and window surrounds. Yellow & blue waves logo).
FQ*	BR Railfreight (Grey bodyside, yellow cabs, red buffer beam/stripe at solebar level, large double-arrow logo).
FR	Fragonset Railways (Black with silver roof and a red bodyside band lined out in white).
FX	Felixstowe Dock & Railway Company (Blue, with a green stripe picked out in white).

FY	Foster Yeoman (Blue/silver. Cast numberplates).
G*	BR (Plain green, with white stripe on main line locomotives).
GB	GB Railfreight (Details awaited).
GG*	BR (Two-tone green).
GL	First Great Western (Green with gold stripe).
GN	Great North Eastern Railway (Dark blue with a red stripe).
GS	Great Scottish & Western Railway (Maroon).
GW*	Great Western Railway (Green, lined out in black & orange. Cast numberplates).
GX	Gatwick Express (Dark grey/white/burgundy/white).
GY	Eurotunnel (Grey and yellow).
HA	Hanson Quarry Products (Dark blue and silver).
HB*	Hunslet-Barclay (Two-tone grey with red solebar).
I*	BR InterCity (Dark grey/white/red/light grey and yellow lower cabsides).
IM*	BR Mainline (Dark grey/white/red/light grey).
IS*	BR InterCity Swallow (Dark grey/white/red/white).
LH*	BR Loadhaul (Black with orange cabsides).
MA	Maintrain (Light blue).
MD	Ministry of Defence (Black).
MG*	BR Mainline Freight (Two-tone grey with black cab doors and window surrounds).
ML*	BR Mainline Freight (Aircraft blue with silver stripe).
MM	Midland Main Line (Teal green with cream lower body sides and three orange stripes).
MR	Mendip Rail (Green, red & silver).
MS*	Mersey Travel departmental (Yellow/black).
N*	BR Network South East (Grey/white/red/white/blue/white).
O	Non standard liveries (See class heading for details).
P	Porterbrook Leasing Company (Purple & grey).
PC*	Pullman Car Company (Umber & cream with gold lettering).
R*	Plain red.
RF*	RFS (E) (Light grey with yellow and blue stripes).
RG*	BR Parcels (Dark grey and red).
RL	RMS Locotech (Blue & red).
RP	Royal Train (Claret, lined out in red and black).
RR*	Regional Railways (Dark Blue/Grey with light blue & white stripes, three narrow dark blue stripes at cab ends).
RT	RT Rail (Black, lined out in red).
RX	Rail Express Systems (Dark grey and red with blue markings).
SB*	Belgian National Railways (SNCB/NMBS-style blue with yellow stripes).
SL	Silverlink (Indigo blue with white stripe, green lower body & yellow doors).
SS	ScotRail Caledonian Sleepers (Two-tone purple with silver stripe).
T*	Transrail (Two-tone grey with Transrail logos).
TC*	BR Engineers/Transrail. (Yellow & grey with black cab doors and window surrounds. Transrail logo).
V	Virgin Trains (Red & grey with three white stripes).
VP	Virgin Trains (Black with a large black & white chequered flag on the bodyside).

WA	Wabtec Rail (Black).
WL*	Waterman Railways (Black with cream and red lining).
WN	West Anglia Great Northern Railway (White with blue, grey and orange stripes).
Y	Plain yellow.
YO*	Foster Yeoman (Blue/silver/blue. Cast numberplates).

OWNER CODES

Code	Owner
50	The Fifty Fund.
90	Deltic 9000 Locomotives Ltd..
A	Angel Trains.
AD	Adtranz (DaimlerChrysler Rail Systems UK).
AM	Alstom Ltd.
AR	Anglia Railways Train Services Ltd.
CA	Cardiff Railway Company Ltd.
CM	Cambrian Trains Ltd.
CN	The Carriage & Traction Company Ltd.
DP	The Deltic Preservation Society Ltd.
DR	Direct Rail Services Ltd.
E	English Welsh & Scottish Railway Ltd.
EF	EWS Finance Ltd.
EN	Enron Teesside Operations Ltd.
ET	Eurotunnel PLC.
EU	Eurostar (UK) Ltd.
FL	Freightliner Ltd.
FR	Fragonset Railways Ltd.
FW	Great Western Trains Company Ltd.
FX	The Felixstowe Dock & Railway Company Ltd.
FY	Foster Yeoman Ltd.
H	HSBC Rail (UK) Ltd.
HA	The Hanson Group Ltd.
HJ	Howard Johnston Engineering.
HL	Heritage Traction Leasing Ltd.
HN	Harry Needle Railroad Company Ltd.
HS	Harry Schneider.
IR	Ian Riley Engineering.
JK	Dr. John Kennedy.
LU	London Underground Ltd.
LW	London & North Western Railway Company Ltd.
MA	Maintrain Ltd.
MD	Ministry of Defence.
ME	Merseyrail Electrics Ltd.
NY	North Yorkshire Moors Railway.
P	Porterbrook Leasing Company Ltd.
PD	Project Defiance Limited.
PO	Privately owned (owner undisclosed).

RC	Railcare Ltd.
RK	Railtrack PLC.
RL	RMS Locotech Ltd.
RT	RT Rail Tours Ltd.
RV	Riviera Trains Ltd.
SA	Sea Containers Railway Services Ltd.
SC	Connex South Central.
SF	SNCF (Société Nayionale des Chemins de fer Français).
SO	Serco Railtest Ltd.
SW	South West Trains Ltd.
VW	West Coast Trains Ltd.
WA	Wabtec Rail.
WF	Western Falcon Rail.
WN	West Anglia Great Northern Railway Ltd.
X	Sold for scrap, awaiting collection or disposal.

POOL CODES

Code	Pool
CDJD	Serco Railtest. Class 08.
CTLO	Cambrian Trains. Operational Fleet.
DFFT	Freightliner. Class 47 with 'Dock Mode'.
DFGC	Freightliner. Class 86/5.
DFGM	Freightliner. Class 66/5, general traffic.
DFHH	Freightliner. Class 66/5, Heavy Haul Division.
DFHZ	Freightliner. Class 57 (standard fuel capacity).
DFLC	Freightliner. Class 90/1.
DFLM	Freightliner. Class 47 (with multiple working equipment).
DFLS	Freightliner. Class 08.
DFLT	Freightliner. Class 47.
DFNC	Freightliner. Class 86/6.
DFRT	Freightliner. Class 66/5, Railtrack contract.
DFTZ	Freightliner. Class 57 (additional fuel capacity).
DHLT	Freightliner. Locomotives awaiting maintenance/repair.
GPSN	Eurostar (UK). Class 73.
GPSS	Eurostar (UK). Class 08.
GPSV	Eurostar (UK). Class 37.
HASS	ScotRail. Class 08.
HEXX	Merseyrail Electrics. Stored.
HFSL	Virgin Cross Country. Class 08.
HFSN	Virgin West Coast. Class 08.
HGSS	Maintrain. Class 08 (Tyseley)
HISE	Maintrain. Class 08 (Derby).
HISL	Maintrain. Class 08 (Neville Hill).
HJSE	First Great Western. Class 08 (Landore).
HJSL	First Great Western. Class 08 (Laira).
HJXX	First Great Western. Class 08 (Old Oak HST & St. Phillips Marsh).
HLSV	Cardiff Railway Company. Class 08. Hire locomotive.
HNRL	Harry Needle Railtrack Leasing. Hire locomotives.

H.P.XX	Silverlink Train Services. Unspecified.
HQXX	West Anglia Great Northern Railway. Class 03.
HSSN	Anglia Railways. Class 08.
HWSU	Connex South Central. Class 09.
HWXX	Connex South Central. Stored.
HYSB	South West Trains. Class 73.
IANA	Anglia Railways. Class 86.
ICCA	Virgin Cross Country. Class 86.
ICCP	Virgin Cross Country. Class 43.
IECA	Great North Eastern Railway. Class 91.
IECB	Great North Eastern Railway. Class 89.
IECP	Great North Eastern Railway. Class 43.
ILRA	Virgin Cross Country. Class 47.
IMLP	Midland Mainline. Class 43.
IVGA	Gatwick Express. Class 73/2.
IWCA	Virgin West Coast. Classes 87 & 90.
IWCP	Virgin West Coast. Class 43.
IWLA	First Great Western. Class 47.
IWPA	Virgin West Coast. Class 86.
IWRP	First Great Western. Class 43.
KCSI	Adtranz. Class 08 (Ilford).
KDSD	Adtranz. Class 08 (Doncaster).
KESE	Alstom. Class 08 (Eastleigh).
KGSS	Railcare. Class 08 (Glasgow).
KWSW	Railcare. Class 08 (Wolverton).
MBDL	Non TOC owned diesel locomotives.
MBEL	Non TOC owned electric locomotives.
QXXX	Railtrack.
RTLO	Riviera Trains. Operational Fleet.
SAXL	HSBC Rail (UK). Off lease.
SBXL	Porterbrook Leasing. Off lease.
SCXL	Angel Trains. Off lease.
SDFR	Fragonset Railways. Operational locomotives.
WAAK	EWS. Class 67.
WBAH	EWS. Class 66 Anglia & Southern.
WBAI	EWS. Class 66 North Eastern (South).
WBAK	EWS. Class 66 Great Western.
WBAM	EWS. Class 66 Scotland, non-RETB equipped.
WBAN	EWS. Class 66 Midland.
WBAT	EWS. Class 66 North Eastern (North).
WBBM	EWS. Class 66 RETB equipped.
WCAI	EWS. Class 60 North Eastern (South).
WCAK	EWS. Class 60 Great Western.
WCAN	EWS. Class 60 Midland.
WCAT	EWS. Class 60 North Eastern (North).
WDAG	EWS. Class 59/2.
WEFE	EWS. Class 90 Freight.
WEOE	EWS. Class 86.
WEPE	EWS. Class 90 Royal Mail & Passenger.
WFAN	EWS. Class 58.
WGAI	EWS. Class 56 North Eastern (South).

WGAT	EWS. Class 56 North Eastern (North).
WHCD	EWS. Class 47.
WHCM	EWS. Class 47 Hired to ScotRail.
WHPT	EWS. New locomotives (pre-acceptance).
WHRD	EWS. Class 47 Special Trains.
WHTD	EWS. Class 47 Hired to Serco Railtest.
WHZX	EWS. Locomotives awaiting disposal.
WKAC	EWS. Class 37 Anglia & Southern.
WKAD	EWS. Class 37 Midlands & North West.
WKCD	EWS. Class 37/4 Hired to First North Western & Cardiff Railway.
WKGS	EWS. Class 37 Identified for possible hire to Spain.
WKBM	EWS. Class 37 RETB equipped.
WKSN	EWS. Class 37 Railtrack Sandite contract.
WMAC	EWS. Class 31.
WNWX	EWS. Main line locomotives – strategic reserve.
WNXX	EWS. Main line locomotives – stored.
WNYX	EWS. Main line locomotives – authorised for component recovery.
WNZX	EWS. Main line locomotives – awaiting disposal.
WPAG	EWS. Class 73.
WTAE	EWS. Class 92 Dollands Moor–Wembley–Mossend–Doncaster & Crewe–Trafford Park Routes.
WTWE	EWS. Class 92 Eurotunnel only.
XHSD	Direct Rail Services. Operational locomotives.
XHSS	Direct Rail Services. Stored locomotives.
XYPA	Mendip Rail. Class 59/0.
XYPO	Mendip Rail. Class 59/1.
XYPS	Mendip Rail. Shunting locomotives.

DEPOT, WORKS & LOCATION CODES

* denotes unofficial code.

Code	Location	Depot Operator
AN	Allerton (Liverpool) T&RSMD	EWS
AY	Ayr SD	EWS
BD	Birkenhead North T&RSMD	Merseyrail Electrics
BH	Barrow Hill	Harry Needle Railroad Company
BG*	Billingham TMD	Enron Teesside Operations
BI	Brighton T&RSMD	Connex South Central
BK	Barton Hill (Bristol) T&RSMD	EWS
BM	Bournemouth T&RSMD	South West Trains
BN	Bounds Green (London) T&RSMD	Great North Eastern Railway
BQ	Bury	East Lancashire Railway
BS	Bescot (Walsall) TMD	EWS
BW*	Barry WRD (closed)	Storage location only

BY	Bletchley T&RSMD	Silverlink Train Services
BZ	St. Blazey (Par) T&RSMD	EWS
CB*	Crewe Basford Hall Yard	Storage location only
CD	Crewe Diesel TMD	EWS
CE	Crewe International Electric T&RSMD	EWS
CF	Cardiff Canton (Loco) TMD	EWS
CG*	Crewe Gresty Lane Sidings	Storage location only
CL	Carlisle Upperby CARMD(closed)	Storage location only
CO	Coquelles (France)	Eurotunnel
CP	Crewe Carriage T&RSMD	London & North Western Railway
CQ	Crewe (The Railway Age) T&RSMD	Carriage & Traction Company
CS	Carnforth T&RSMD	West Coast Railway Company
CT*	Chester WRD (closed)	Storage location only
CU*	Carlisle Currock WRD (closed)	Storage location only
CW*	Crewe South Yard	Storage location only
DD*	Doncaster Wood Yard	Storage location only.
DE*	Dewsbury	RMS Locotech
DI	Didcot SD	EWS
DR	Doncaster TMD	EWS
DY	Derby Etches Park T&RSMD	Maintrain
EC	Edinburgh Craigentinny T&RSMD	Great North Eastern Railway
EH	Eastleigh TMD	EWS
FB	Ferrybridge T&RSMD	EWS
FD	Unallocated	Freightliner
FE	Unallocated	Freightliner
FW	Fort William	EWS
FX*	Felixstowe TMD	Felixstowe Dock & Railway Company
GD	Gateshead WRD (closed)	Storage location only
HE	Hornsey T&RSMD	West Anglia Great Northern
HG	Hither Green TMD	EWS
HM	Healey Mills (Wakefield) SD	EWS
IM	Immingham TMD	EWS
IS	Inverness T&RSMD	ScotRail
IW*	Ipswich WRD	Storage location only
KD	Carlisle Kingmoor TMD	Direct Rail Services
KK	Kirkdale SD	Merseyrail Electrics
KN	MOD Kineton	Ministry of Defence
KR	Kidderminster	Severn Valley Railway
KY	Knottingley T&RSMD	EWS
LA	Laira (Plymouth) T&RSMD	First Great Western
LB	Loughborough	Brush Traction
LE	Landore (Swansea) T&RSMD	First Great Western
LG	Longsight Electric (Manchester) T&RSMD	Cross Fleet
LO	Longsight Diesel (Manchester) TMD	First North Western
LR	Leicester SD	EWS
MD	Merehead TMD	Mendip Rail
MG	Margam (Port Talbot) SD	EWS
MH	Millerhill (Edinburgh) SD	EWS
ML	Motherwell TMD	EWS
NC	Norwich Crown Point T&RSMD	Anglia Railways
NL	Neville Hill InterCity (Leeds) T&RSMD	Maintrain

NP	North Pole International (London) T&RSMD	Eurostar (UK)
NY	Grosmont T&RSMD	North Yorkshire Moors Railway
OC	Old Oak Common (London) TMD	EWS
OM	Old Oak Common (London) CARMD	First Great Western
OO	Old Oak Common HST T&RSMD (London)	First Great Western
PM	St. Phillips Marsh (Bristol) T&RSMD	First Great Western
PY*	MOD Pig's Bay (Shoeburyness)	Storage location only
RL	Ropley	Mid Hants Railway
SD	Sellafield T&RSMD	Direct Rail Services
SF	Stratford (London) SD	EWS
SL	Stewarts Lane (London) T&RSMD	Gatwick Express
ST*	Southampton Maritime SD	Freightliner
SP	Springs Branch (Wigan) CRDC	EWS
SU	Selhurst (Croydon) T&RSMD	Connex South Central
TE	Thornaby T&RSMD	EWS
TM	Birmingham Railway Museum	Birmingham Railway Museum/Fragonset Railways
TO	Toton (Nottinghamshire) TMD	EWS
TS	Tyseley (Birmingham) T&RSMD	Maintrain
TT*	Toton Training School (Notts)	Storage location only
TY	Tyne Yard	EWS
WA	Warrington Arpley SD	EWS
WN	Willesden (London) TMD	West Coast Train Care
WR*	West Ruislip	London Underground
ZA	Railway Technical Centre, Derby	Serco Railtest/AEA Technology/Fragonset Railways
ZB	Doncaster	Wabtec
ZC	Crewe	Adtranz
ZE*	Washwood Heath (Birmingham)	Alstom
ZF	Doncaster	Adtranz
ZG	Eastleigh	Alstom
ZH	Glasgow	Railcare
ZI	Ilford	Adtranz
ZN	Wolverton	Railcare

DEPOT TYPE CODES

CARMD	Carriage Maintenance Depot
CRDC	Component Recovery & Disposal Centre
CSD	Carriage Servicing Depot
CS	Carriage Sidings.
SD	Servicing Depot
TMD	Traction Maintenance Depot
T&RSMD	Traction & Rolling Stock Depot
WRD	Wagon Repair Depot.